THE REMINISCENCES OF
Dr. Leo M. Karpeles

INTERVIEWED BY
Paul Stillwell

U.S. Naval Institute • Annapolis, Maryland

Copyright © 1996

Preface

This oral history grew out of a request last year from Mr. Arsen Charles, museum curator for the Boston National Historical Park at the former Charlestown Navy Yard. He indicated that Dr. Karpeles, who now lives in Annapolis, had worked at the Boston Navy Yard as a civilian physicist in World War II. Specifically, he was involved in deperming warships to improve their protection against magnetic mines. Mr. Charles asked that the Naval Institute interview Dr. Karpeles as a means of adding to the knowledge of the shipyard's work during the war.

I agreed to conduct the interview on behalf of Boston's historical park, because it would add to the Naval Institute's collection of memoirs in areas not well covered previously. We have little on magnetic mine defenses and on civilian employees of the Navy. Dr. Karpeles was gracious in his cooperation, talking not only about his wartime experiences in Boston but also those in Hawaii and as a member of the crew of the battleship Alabama. In telling his life story, Dr. Karpeles explained the circumstances by which he became first a physicist, then a physician. During the interview, he displayed a healthy sense of cynicism when warranted and a high degree of patriotism throughout. His contribution to the material available on World War II is a welcome one.

In the completion of this transcript, Dr. Karpeles and I have done some editing in the interests of smoothness and clarity. Ms. Ann Hassinger of the Naval Institute's history division has made a significant contribution through her diligence in the overall process of printing, proofreading, and overseeing the binding.

Paul Stillwell
Director, History Division
U.S. Naval Institute
August 1996

DR. LEO M. KARPELES

Born: 29 May 1920, Washington, D.C.

Graduated, Central High School, Washington, D.C., 1937

Graduated, University of North Carolina, Chapel Hill, North Carolina, 1941, B.S. in physics

Teaching assistant and graduate student in physics, Carnegie Institute of Technology, Pittsburgh, Pennsylvania, one semester in 1941-42; no degree

Contract physicist, Navy Bureau of Ordnance, 1941-43, degaussing and acoustic mine countermeasures and development, Washington, D.C; Boston, Massachusetts; Pearl Harbor, Hawaii

Civil Service physicist, grade P-2, degaussing and acoustic mine countermeasures for the Bureau of Ordnance, 1943-45, Pearl Harbor, Hawaii, and San Diego, California

Drafted May 1945 as seaman first class into radio technician school. Released from technician school in late 1945 and transferred to the USS Alabama (BB-60). Advanced to electrician's mate third class in early 1946. Honorable discharge, July 1946

Graduate student in physics, Johns Hopkins University, Baltimore, Maryland, 1946-47; no degree

Service engineer, General Electric X-ray Corporation, Seattle, Washington, 1946-47

Electronic Engineer, 13th Coast Guard District, Civil Service, grade P-2, 1947-50

Student, University of Washington School of Medicine, Seattle, Washington, 1950-55, M.D. in 1955

"Rotating" intern, Albany Hospital, Albany, New York, 1955-56

Postdoctoral fellow (NIH), Department of Physiology and Biophysics, University of Washington, 1956-58

Research instructor, Department of Physiology and Biophysics, University of Washington, 1958-60

Assistant Professor, Physiology Department, University of Maryland Medical School, Baltimore, Maryland, 1960-66

Associate Professor, Physiology Department, University of Maryland Medical School, 1966-78; retired following sabbatical, 1978

Resident, University of Maryland, Department of Family Practice, 1977-80

Licensed in family practice, Blue Ridge Summit, Pennsylvania, with full medical privileges at Waynesboro, Pennsylvania, Hospital, 1980-86

Retired, 1986

Additional work experience: as a farm hand and stable hand during high school; about 12 months, 1938-41, as a student assistant at the U.S. Bureau of Standards, in the engineering mechanics and radio divisions; a month or so in 1946 as an unpaid assistant in the Cancer Institute of the National Institutes of Health; 12 months in 1951-52 as a GS-9 physicist for the Veterans Administration Hospital in Seattle, Washington

Married to: the former Eileen Burrer, 1953 to 1970; the former Nancy Sarles, 1986-present

Children--three daughters: Katherine, born in 1953; Robin, born in 1955; and Tamia, born in 1957

Authorization

The U.S. Naval Institute is hereby authorized to make available to individuals, libraries, and other repositories of its choosing the transcripts of one oral history interview concerning the life and career of the undersigned. The interview was recorded on 30 May 1995 in collaboration with Paul Stillwell for the U.S. Naval Institute.

The undersigned does hereby release and assign to the U.S. Naval Institute all right, title, restrictions, and interest in the interviews. The copyright in both the oral and transcribed versions shall be the sole property of the U.S. Naval Institute. The tape recordings of the interviews are and will remain the property of the U.S. Naval Institute.

Signed and sealed this _Third_ day of _June_ 1995.

Leo M. Karpeles
Leo M. Karpeles

Interview with Dr. Leo M. Karpeles

Place: Dr. Karpeles's home, Annapolis, Maryland

Date: Tuesday, 30 May 1995

Interviewer: Paul Stillwell

Q: I wonder if you could please start with a little background at the beginning on your education and what you had done before you got involved with the Navy.

Dr. Karpeles: All right. When I got involved with the Navy, I was 21. I graduated from the University of North Carolina with a bachelor's degree in physics in June of '41. Then I went to Carnegie Tech as a teaching assistant and had been there a few months when the United States entered the war.* I had all the patriotic fervor of a 21 year old, but I didn't imagine that somebody with a degree in physics ought to go and enlist in the ground troops. I lived in Washington at the time, so on my Christmas vacation I very naively just sort of made the rounds of the military offices in Washington. I said, "I've got a degree in physics, and I think I ought to be doing something in the war effort."

Q: Was this a few weeks after Pearl Harbor was attacked?

Dr. Karpeles: Yes, and most of the people I talked to were recruiting sergeants or somebody like that. The typical reaction was, "What's a physicist? Never heard of that."

Q: What was your draft status at that point?

Dr. Karpeles: I don't remember for sure, but I was probably on a student deferment because of my work at Carnegie Tech.

---

* Carnegie Institute of Technology, Pittsburgh, Pennsylvania.

Q: Were you pursuing postgraduate education there?

Dr. Karpeles: Yes. I was involved in some work in infrared and some work with molecular beams. This work probably had no military application, but my mentors at Carnegie Tech were very distressed to hear I was thinking of finding war work. They assured me that it would be only a matter of months before Carnegie Tech would be getting military contracts, and they would need me there. Somehow it seemed to me that they were telling me that I didn't need to change my life-style at all. I could ride this war out just fine right where I was, and that didn't feel right to me.

Q: They had a selfish motivation for wanting to keep you there.

Dr. Karpeles: Of course they did, and yet they may well have been right. It's quite possible that one way or another I could have done more for the war effort if I had just sat tight. I could have helped with whatever research contracts they would have gotten from the military and also advanced my own skill above the level of a bachelor's degree.

Q: Did you go to all the services or just the Navy?

Dr. Karpeles: I know I went to the Army Signal Corps, and I probably was just kind of using the phone book or something to look for places to go. I wasn't clever at all. I went into one of the old temporary buildings that had been built down on D Street during World War I. They were was still functioning for World War II. By this time I was getting sort of uncomfortable about going into these places and applying, but I walked in and said I was a physicist and looking for a job. Suddenly I got the "Right this way, sir" treatment.

Q: What was the source of your discomfort at that point?

Dr. Karpeles: That people seemed to think I was some kind of a kook. I suppose there were a lot of guys going into recruiting offices and volunteering, and there were a lot of guys trying to figure out how to make a fast buck. But all I was doing was trying to figure out how to use my skills to the advantage of the military operation we were getting into.

Q: Were you proposing to go in uniform, or did you want to do this as a civilian?

Dr. Karpeles: I was just proposing to go. I didn't think they wanted me just to enlist in the ranks, but I would have gone in any uniform.

Q: But essentially you were suggesting you could be more useful in the physicist's role.

Dr. Karpeles: Exactly. So finally I came to this place where they knew at least something of what a physicist was. I inferred that they must have had some kind of directive to latch on to anybody that looked like a physicist, because there just wasn't any discussion about it. They didn't ask to see transcripts or recommendations or anything that said I had a degree in physics from the University of North Carolina. They said, "Do you want to go to work?"

I said, "Well, that's why I'm here." I was introduced to a Lieutenant Kirtley, who was assigned to the Bureau of Ordnance.[*]

Q: Was this at the Main Navy Department Building on Constitution?

Dr. Karpeles: No, that was a big white-front building. The War Department and the Navy Department were side by side. Then, on down Constitution Avenue--as I recall, it was D Street--there were these low, gray stucco buildings that surely had only been intended to stay up for only a few years. But nobody had ever found the time or money or whatever to get rid of them, and so they were back in use.

---

[*] Lieutenant Charles A. Kirtley, USN (Ret.).

Q: Did you have a feeling for why Lieutenant Kirtley was more sympathetic or more interested in your suggestion than the other offices you tried?

Dr. Karpeles: Well, as I said, I just got this sense that he was hiring anybody that even looked like a physicist.

Q: You had finally managed to make a connection with the right office.

Dr. Karpeles: I finally got into an office where they had an idea what a physicist was. What he was doing was lining people up to go into degaussing work. I don't really know this at all, but I suspect his function was just to find people and get them on the payroll, because after he had me on the payroll he didn't have anything for me to do. They hired me on a procurement contract rather than an employment contract.

Q: Did you have to go through any Civil Service screening or tests?

Dr. Karpeles: No, no. It was a procurement contract. As I gathered, it was the same sort of thing they would have written if they were buying 100 typewriters. The contract said that I would be paid $7.00 a day. This was a concession because I had a little graduate work. If I hadn't had any graduate experience, it would have been $6.00 a day, but I didn't care.

Q: Well, I think you were making more at that point than a newly commissioned ensign, so that was appropriate.[*]

Dr. Karpeles: At $7.00 a day I was probably getting what a jaygee would have made.[†] In any event, it was adequate to the time. The government Civil Service was paying $2,000 a

---

[*] In early 1942 an ensign received annual base pay of $1,500, plus rental and subsistence allowances totaling $699.00.
[†] Jaygee--lieutenant (junior grade).

year, which was slightly more, but there was a lot of red tape connected with that, and anyhow Civil Service wasn't offering me anything.

Q: Did the procurement contract affect your draft exemption?

Dr. Karpeles: It did, and I never asked at all. I was perfectly willing to put on the uniform. I was willing to help. Lieutenant Kirtley asked me where I would want to work, and I said, "Well, my home's in Washington. I'd be delighted to work in Washington, but I'm not putting any restrictions on. My object is to be useful. I'll work anywhere."

Q: Had you grown up in Washington before going to North Carolina?

Dr. Karpeles: Yes.

Q: So you didn't have the hassles other people did in finding a place to live.

Dr. Karpeles: No. There was no problem about a place to live. But he simply put me at a desk and asked somebody to give me something to do. They gave me some tracings of ship hulls on which one had to add the locations of coils.

Q: In discussing your work with mines, let me ask whether you use the words deperming and degaussing interchangeably.

Dr. Karpeles: No. Degaussing is a broader term. It covers everything that you do to a ship to protect it against magnetic mines. There were some misconceptions about magnetic mines. For instance, they aren't attracted to the ship, as news articles were reporting at that time. They are simply fired by the ship as its magnetic field passes close to the mine. But because they can be configured to lie on the bottom in shallow water, they can be much more powerful than the contact mines. The result is that they can sink a ship at the range of several hundred feet. So they were pretty devastating instruments, particularly before anybody really knew what they were.

I suppose it was sometime in 1941 that the British had succeeded in figuring out what these armaments were that had been destroying their merchant fleet. They knew that the mines would trip magnetically, and that was about all they knew. The object of degaussing was to get the magnetic fields of ships down as low as possible.

The reason there are various elements of degaussing is that the ship carries permanent magnetism which is hammered into it when it's on the ways, being built, as well as magnetism induced by the earth's magnetic field when the ship is in operation. For some reason, it seems that practically all the ways that the Navy was using in shipyards were on a north-south heading, so practically all the ships had a north pole on the bow. Also, because the magnetic field of the earth dips fairly sharply in the northern hemisphere they had a north pole in the keel. Deperming was an effort to neutralize that field which had been built in when the ship was being built. The deperming was very clumsy and unsuccessful in 1941 and '42 but became much better later in the war.

Q: Had any of your studies specifically dealt with magnetism?

Dr. Karpeles: In the sense that the physics course at Carolina was a fairly intensive basic program. There was a course in electricity and magnetism, there was a course in radio and electronics, there was a course in acoustics, a course in mechanics, and so forth and so on. Each of these things was compartmentalized, and so I knew the basic principles of electromagnetism quite well. I really didn't know anything advanced, but neither did anybody else that I came in contact with.

I started talking about degaussing, and I talked about deperming--getting the permanent field out of the ship which was associated with the ship's having been built. The other field that you had to deal with was the field that is induced in the ship at all times, wherever it goes in the earth's magnetic field. Of course, that field changes every time the ship changes latitude, and it changes every time the ship changes heading. So it had to be neutralized by coils that were installed in the ship. Through these coils the current could be adjusted frequently as the ship changed heading or changed latitude.

So what I was doing there in Washington was tracing in the locations of coils. I used as my guide installations that had already been made in the same class of ships, so that it was an idiot job. You just looked at this picture, transposed it to that picture, and you were done. I didn't have much of that.

Q: Where was that work taking place?

Dr. Karpeles: It was at this temporary building on D Street. I did everything they gave me to do, but it didn't take very long. I got terribly bored, so I went out and bought a newspaper and started reading it in the office. Somebody came around and said, "You can't do that."

I said, "Well, I've done everything I've been given to do. I don't know what else to do."

"Well, you can't be reading newspapers. It would look terrible if somebody came through here. You've got to stay busy."

"Busy doing what?"

"Well, anything, just stay busy."

Well, there was something else I could do. They did have a lot of restricted publications about degaussing, and I could read them. But there wasn't much to them. It didn't take long to do that, and so I was still in this bind. I didn't have to be busy, but I had to look busy. So I went around looking for anybody who seemed to have any work to do. The only people that had any work to do were the file clerks. They were busy, so I went back in the file room and said, "Do you want some help with the filing?" They were delighted. So I helped them with the filing.

Q: What sort of files were those?

Dr. Karpeles: God knows! Correspondence and these diagrams that I'd been working on--things like that. I hadn't been at that more than a few hours before somebody with some authority came back and said, "You can't do this."

I said, "Why not?"

"Well, it's not right. You're back here with all these file clerks." I think he thought it was a wonderful opportunity for hanky-panky, and he assumed that I was going to be carrying on behind the file cabinets somewhere.

Q: What month was that?

Dr. Karpeles: I went back and finished my quarter at Carnegie Tech, and I believe it was February 1 that I went to work at the Bureau of Ordnance. After I had worked there for several weeks--or tried to look busy for several weeks--I got travel orders to go to Boston. I believe this was still February, because it was cold as the dickens in Boston. I remember that.

I didn't know anything about travel orders. They said, "These are your travel orders and you present them when you get to Boston Navy Yard."

So I went to the gate of the Boston Navy Yard and said, "I've got these travel orders," and the Marine, I guess, probably sent me to the correct office.

Q: Were you leaving behind another group of physicists who were doing what you had been doing?

Dr. Karpeles: Yes. Pretty much the place was full of people who had been hired in this title of physicist, and they were all trying to look busy.

Q: How many would you guess there were?

Dr. Karpeles: Somewhere between a dozen and 20.

Q: Did you commune with them about this frustration you were experiencing?

Dr. Karpeles: I don't remember that I did. I think they'd all been there longer than I and had adapted better than I. They seemed to be happy.

Q: Maybe it suited them better to do nothing.

Dr. Karpeles: I suppose, but most of them were not physicists except by act of the United States Government. If you had a degree in chemistry or mathematics or biology or anything that sounded technical, they would call you a physicist and hire you.

Anyhow, when I got to Boston things were different. There was a lot of work to be done. As I think about it in my cynicism now, the work was coming in when the day laborers split off. They would get time and a half for overtime, so they went off promptly at 3:00 P.M. By some coincidence the ships that needed deperming would show up at about 2:30 P.M., and we'd go down and work on them till midnight or 1:00 A.M. or whatever it took.

Q: You and how many other people were involved?

Dr. Karpeles: Oh, I suppose there were four or five physicists and some junior officers and a whole crew of riggers, because we needed riggers to put the cables on the ships.

Q: Had the other physicists come in essentially as you had, on a contract basis?

Dr. Karpeles: Yes, they were all on contract. Where they had all come from and that sort of thing I can't tell you, but we were all on contract.

Q: One more question about Washington, please. The Navy was just then starting at the Naval Gun Factory a mine disposal school. Did you have any contact with that organization?

Dr. Karpeles: I knew nothing about it. It would have scared the hell out of me if I'd been involved with that. Anyhow, as I say, I was in a heroic frame of mind. I probably would have got myself blown up if it came to that.

In Boston we did this deperming activity and, as I say, it tended to start in the midafternoon and run into the night. Nobody seemed to care what hours I kept as long as I was there when they needed me. So my practice was to finish at whatever hour of the night I finished, go home and take a bath and get in bed, get eight hours' sleep, get up, get my breakfast, go back to the Navy yard whatever time that happened to be. Apparently that was completely okay. In fact, I was told by some of the guys I was working with that the kind of contract we had if you worked past midnight you were already paid for the next day. Since you had already worked that next day, you didn't need to come in at all. But I had nothing else to do, for that matter.

Q: Where were you living?

Dr. Karpeles: The Navy sent me on subsistence, $6.00 a day. At that rate things probably would have been tight if I'd stayed at a hotel, and they probably thought I would stay at a hotel. But I found a very nice room on Beacon Hill--in fact on Beacon Street. It cost me a whole $10.00 a week, but with $6.00 a day subsistence that wasn't a problem. So basically all the time I was in Boston I was banking my $7.00 pay and living on my $6.00 subsistence. It was pretty soft in that respect.

Pretty much I was at the Navy yard all the time I wasn't home eating and sleeping, though I do remember there was a gal in the same rooming house with me, and I took her out a couple times. She had a boyfriend somewhere, and I had a girlfriend somewhere, and we both agreed that this was strictly for company--somebody to go out with. We were both very nice kids and didn't do any of the things kids would have done today.

Q: Well, it was convenient for both of you.

Dr. Karpeles: It was fun for both of us. But, as I recall, my recreation time wasn't very much, primarily because I thought I ought to go to the yard as soon after I got up as was convenient. I usually didn't get off at the yard until close to midnight one way or the other. So that's the way we worked.

Q: What about the transportation arrangements to and from work?

Dr. Karpeles: I asked my landlady how to get to the Charlestown Navy Yard, and she told me to go down to the Charles Street subway station, get a train to take you down to Park Square or something like that, a transfer point downtown.[*] There I was to get such and such a train--I don't remember what it was anymore--and it would take me to such and such a station near the Navy yard. So I did that for about a week. Then, one way or another, I got hold of a map of Boston and found out that I was riding all over town to get to a place that was about a mile and a half away. [Laughter] After that I just walked over there. I was enjoying that walk.

Q: What went on in those nine hours or so that you put in between 3:00 o'clock and midnight?

Dr. Karpeles: The ships would range up to the size of a destroyer. Most of them were destroyers or destroyer escorts. A few of them were minesweepers, and a few were cargo vessels.

The process involved getting a solenoid, which was essentially a spiral, wrapped around the entire ship, stem to stern, under the keel and over the superstructure from one end of the ship to the other. This was done by taking lengths of cable long enough to reach from the gunwale on one side to the gunwale on the other and dipping the loop under the bow of the ship and walking back along the two rails to wherever we wanted this coil to be positioned and then lashing it with marlin to the rails there.

---

[*] Charlestown was an independent city until it became part of Boston in 1874. It was the site of the Boston Navy Yard, which was eventually closed in the 1970s.

Q: How many of these would you have along the length of the ship?

Dr. Karpeles: I'd say 20 or 30--that order of magnitude. After you got the ones under the ship, you could carry the ones over relatively easily and connect them up so that the whole coil was in series. One of the coils that went over the ship would connect to the one that went under the ship, connected to the next frame forward, and so forth. So you'd have the whole ship wrapped with this coil.

Q: Was this a process that was done during construction for later ships?

Dr. Karpeles: No. It was always done after the ship was commissioned. We were doing it at Pearl Harbor all through the war. None of these processes lasted forever. The magnetism that was inherent in the ship would overcome the magnetism we slammed into it with these coils. When we started, the result of our efforts lasted for a period of hours, and when we got good at it for a period of months. But the ships had to be repeatedly depermed. We measured the effects of the work with what we called the pistol pot magnetometer.

Q: How did that work?

Dr. Karpeles: Well, the basic conception was that if this permeable iron moved inside of a coil and there was a magnetic field where it was moving, the magnetic field would magnetize this permeable iron. Then that magnet moving in the coil would generate a current that you could measure with instruments on deck. So that current that you measured when the iron moved had to be nullified--brought to zero. To do that, you had a second coil around the first coil, and in that second coil you could induce a steady current which would create a magnetic field which could be calculated.

On deck we had one galvanometer that told you whether the motion of that permeable iron was generating any current and another meter that told you how many milliamperes you were putting through the coil that surrounded the inside assembly. That could be translated in terms of how many milligauss you were canceling out with that outer coil. When you had exactly canceled out the milligauss of field that the ship was generating at that point, you would get no deflection of the galvanometer when you moved the movable piece of iron. You moved the movable piece of iron by a very simple suction device which was something like a tire pump. If you jerked up on the handle of the tire pump, that created a suction on the hose that came out of the bottom of it, and that was transmitted down to the magnetometer, which was under the ship and made this little piece of iron jump.

Q: So it was hooked by a long hose?

Dr. Karpeles: Yes. There were two long hoses, one for the magnetometer core and the other to measure the depth at which the pistol pot, as we called it, was positioned. Otherwise, you could make only a rough guess at the depth. We had two pieces of rope that we used to haul the cable back to its position, and we could make a pretty fair guess at the depth by the amount of rope we payed out. But it was going around the hull of the ship, and nobody bothered to try to calculate what depth that would correspond to. So we added the second tire pump, in turn connected to a pressure gauge. When we pushed that tire pump down, the pressure that it took to make air bubble out at the bottom of the hose was reliably indicative of how deep the pistol pot was. The deeper the pistol pot was, the more pressure we had to use to force the air out of the hose. It was really crude stuff.

Q: What was the power source for this operation?

Dr. Karpeles: The power source for the deperming was automobile batteries--by the hundreds. My recollection is that we stored them in a room adjacent to the pier. It was a room nearly as large as this one, and it was quite full of automobile batteries, rack after rack after rack.

Q: Why would you use the batteries rather than taking the power from a generator?

Dr. Karpeles: We needed much more current than you could readily get from a generator. We were using currents at that time of several hundred amperes. Later on, when we got to know better what we were doing, we used several thousand amperes. But by the time we got to that, we were using submarine batteries instead of automobile batteries.

Q: How did you hook that many batteries together so they can accomplish that?

Dr. Karpeles: It wasn't complicated.

Q: Just a lot of wire.

Dr. Karpeles: A lot of wire. Yes, and the wire had to be heavy enough to carry all that current. What we were using was the heaviest gauge of welding cable that was being made at that time, and we were doubling it. It took more than one welding cable to carry the current.

Q: So then would it take just nine hours to do one ship completely?

Dr. Karpeles: Yes, about that. That included wrapping the coils on, going through this measuring process and zapping current through the coils and going through the measuring process again and zapping it again. When we first did it, we just tried to zap it down to zero field. Those ships would go out the next morning and cross a range where the ship's field was measured, and the field would be back again. The magnetic field was at zero at midnight, but by 8:00 o'clock in the morning it already would be back where it had been.

Q: Very frustrating.

Dr. Karpeles: Well. I was a peon. All I had to do was carry out the instructions.

Q: Who was your supervisor?

Dr. Karpeles: I believe it was a lieutenant commander. I don't remember his name though. Anyhow, it wasn't a very high-level officer. I believe he probably wasn't making any decisions. He was probably transmitting information back to Washington, where other people were scratching their heads and saying what to do next.

Q: Were you making some innovations yourself in this process?

Dr. Karpeles: No. The only innovation I was making was in the amount of work I did. The riggers who were doing the work were pretty much time servers and served time as little as possible. I was very gung ho, and I was constantly finding somebody sitting around smoking a cigarette, so I'd say, "Let's go get a cable and take it back." I wasn't supposed to be taking cables back, but until the cables were wrapped I had nothing to do. So I'd be grabbing one end and trying to enlist somebody to grab the other end and take one of these things back and lash it down. Then we'd go back up to the bow, and get another one. The guy I got back here sitting down to rest up, I'd find somebody else to do another one.

Q: Could you enlist the aid of a foreman or leadman or someone else?

Dr. Karpeles: I didn't know enough, and I don't know whether I could have anyhow. Because the attitude of the yard workers was very much "this is a job." When it was time to go off the shift, they had their hands washed and their overalls changed, and they were standing at the head of the gangway. Meanwhile, I was thinking, "We've got this destroyer here. She's probably got $4 million tied up, and she ought to be out." I assumed the whole crew was eager to go out there and destroy something, so we had to get her out tonight. No foolishness about it.

Q: As the days and weeks passed, did you get better measurements to indicate that you were reducing the signature?

Dr. Karpeles: Yes. The first thing that we found was that you needed to reverse the magnetic field. And before you started trying to bring it to zero, you wanted to measure it. You find you've got a field that's plus 400 milligauss, so you hit the batteries until you get it down to minus 400 milligauss, and then from minus 400 milligauss you come up to zero. That would last a week or two.

Q: Why was that better?

Dr. Karpeles: Because, as I understand things and understood them at the time, this magnetism essentially consisted of individual iron molecules that had assumed a particular orientation during the time that the ship was being built. They had a pretty good memory for the orientation that was hammered into them, so we were sort of trying to wipe out that memory by giving them an opposite field to memorize. Then, coming back from that, you could say, "Well, now we've got this poor little molecule confused. It doesn't know where to go, so maybe it will stay where we put it." [Laughter] The principle was sound, but it was not sound enough.

Q: Yes, because you wanted the deperming to last more than a week.

Dr. Karpeles: That's right. A week really wasn't much better than nothing. It was a year later that the Navy finally figured out to do this job right. It took a lot more current, and it took going positive and negative and positive and negative and positive and negative until you gradually homed in on the zero field. In other words, once you got these molecules thoroughly confused, they'd stay put for a good period of months.

Q: Well, and actually didn't the Navy build deperming facilities so that this process would be more than an ad hoc thing?

Dr. Karpeles: Oh, yes, yes. The deperming facility at Pearl Harbor was built for the purpose and was far more effective in every way.

Q: It saved a lot of physical labor in moving those coils.

Dr. Karpeles: Well, they still wrapped coils, but the measurements were made with perhaps 100 or more instruments planted on the bottom of the harbor, rather than four or five on tire pumps. Also, for measurements the magnetometers were balanced by some kind of a servo mechanism that was simple but suitable to the task. The results were printed out on a teletype, so that each time you wanted a measurement you just pushed a button, and after a little period of time the teletype would print you a map of the bottom under the hull, where the ship was moored, showing all the fields through these numbers. If any magnetometer couldn't balance, the machine would print a little row of question marks there.

Q: Did the work in Boston give you satisfaction and fulfill your desire to be involved?

Dr. Karpeles: Yes. I worked hard and thought I was doing something useful. Whether I was or not, I wanted to think I was.

Q: Did you have interaction with the officers and enlisted men in the crews of the ships?

Dr. Karpeles: Hardly any. The only interaction I can remember is asking somebody where the bathroom was and he said, "The what?"

    I said, "The bathroom."

    "What's that?"

    "The men's room."

    "What's that?"

    So finally somebody took pity on me and said, "You're looking for the head."

Q: Do you remember the names of any of the specific ships?

Dr. Karpeles: No, not at all.

Q: Did the crews remain on board while this deperming was taking place?

Dr. Karpeles: I don't know. I think they must have kept a skeleton crew on board; they'd have had to. But from my subsequent Navy experience I would expect they were all on liberty, except whatever they needed for a gangway watch and to keep the engines going and things like that.

Q: I take it then that it wasn't necessary to get the crew members off the ship so they wouldn't be harmed.

Dr. Karpeles: Oh, no. The degaussing wouldn't hurt anybody. I should also say that at that time we were stupid, and we thought that radar wouldn't hurt anybody either. In fact, however, there's some danger connected with being too close to a radar field. Anyhow, we thought we weren't hurting anybody, so we were not worried about that at all.

Q: Would it have any effect if the ship's electronic equipment was operating during this process?

Dr. Karpeles: Now that you mention it, I believe there was a necessity to take the magnetic compasses off. And I believe there probably was a need to take off the flinders bars and the navigator's balls and all that stuff associated with the magnetic compass.* Of course, every electrical instrument on the ship could have a little magnet in it, but we wouldn't demagnetize those. This was a totally different order of magnitude.

---

* Flinders bars are iron bars inserted in the binnacle of a magnetic compass to compensate for deviation. Navigator's balls are large metal balls positioned on either side of the compass.

Q: What would have been the effect if you had performed this while you had the magnetic compass and associated equipment on board?

Dr. Karpeles: I suspect we would have induced some magnetism in the flinders bar and the balls, and the compass would have had to be recalibrated afterwards. In fact, now that I'm remembering, we had people in the office whose job it was to recalibrate the compasses, even though they weren't on board when they demagnetized the ship. The deperming changed the magnetism of the ship, and so the adjustment of the compasses would have to be changed. You're reminding me of things I'd forgotten.

Q: Some of the employees up there in Boston apparently remembered the electrical cables being stretched out in a ropewalk. Did you see that?

Dr. Karpeles: A ropewalk. What's that?

Q: It was a place where they made rope.

Dr. Karpeles: I didn't see it. I probably wouldn't have known a ropewalk if I'd seen one unless somebody said, "This is a ropewalk. Here's what we do." Nobody was doing a guided tour for me, but I don't remember how we had the cables waiting to be used. My first guess would be that they were all flaked out along the dock. That would be the sensible thing to have done, just pick up the two ends and take it.

Q: Maybe they were just stored in this place temporarily.

Dr. Karpeles: It's possible. Or maybe somebody was rounding up some decent cables to replace the welding cables we were using. I don't know.

Q: Did you observe any of the shipbuilding work that was going on there at the time?

Dr. Karpeles: Not really, because, in the first place, I don't know that shipbuilding work was going on at Charlestown Navy Yard. Maybe it was, but you've got to realize I was the guy who asked for a bathroom. I knew nothing about the Navy, and I was busy enough trying to learn what I was supposed to be doing that I didn't get to move around the yard and ask questions like, "Well, what are you guys doing?"

Q: Very focused.

Dr. Karpeles: Very focused. Now, after I got to Pearl Harbor, I took more of an interest in what was going on as time went on. Also, we were seeing real war damage there. It was hard not to get interested in both the damage and the means of repairing and the dry docks that were being built--things like that. It was all very much a part of what everybody was interested in.

Q: Was there more than one place that the deperming was going on, or was it just that one pier where you worked?

Dr. Karpeles: In Charlestown Navy Yard, just the one pier. I'm sure of that. I don't know how many places there may have been on the East Coast at that time, because they really sent me to Boston to learn the trade. It seems like if there'd been a place closer, they'd have sent me someplace closer. But I don't know that either.

Q: You said before we started that this was a pier that couldn't take ships on both sides, on one side only.

Dr. Karpeles: That's right.

Q: Was that because there would be some effect on a ship on the other side of the pier if you had?

Dr. Karpeles: No, I don't think so. I think it was because they needed a place to put the shed with all the batteries in it, and there was not much room on a standard pier for an extra building like that. That's the only basis on which I picked out which pier I thought it was that we were probably working at.

Q: Were there other physicists helping you with this, or was that your baby?

Dr. Karpeles: I think probably on any one job there would have been three of us. At least in the beginning, the crew had to have someone more experienced than I was. There had to be somebody who set the resistance and threw the switch on the deperming current when it was time to shoot it. I didn't do that. And there probably was more than one person taking these pistol pot measurements. So I would guess there were probably three physicists on a job. I would guess there were probably six in the office. I think they called it PR-8D at that time, whatever that meant.

I never knew what the other guys were doing particularly. I tended to assume that everybody knew more than I did. There was another kind of operation that went on. It was called "wiping" submarines, because wrapping coils didn't work well with the submarines for some reason, and so they put a horizontal loop of cable around the vessel, below the waterline, and pulled it up.

Q: Was this cable rigged longitudinally on the submarine?

Dr. Karpeles: Yes. They called that wiping, because when the current was flowing in the cable it would magnetically adhere to the side of the vessel, and so it would sort of wipe the vessel as it came up. We did that a lot at Pearl Harbor, and I think we probably did some at Boston, but I don't remember it definitely.

Q: Did you have one of these ships coming in for this procedure every day?

Dr. Karpeles: My feeling is that it was pretty much every day. It was a rare day we didn't have something. Seems like maybe they'd scrounge up something that could stand to be depermed; I don't know. Of course, they must have had generators running to recharge the batteries all the time that we weren't using them. But I don't remember that either.

Q: Did this procedure get stale after while, doing the same thing every day?

Dr. Karpeles: I suppose it would have. I was there for two months. I had 30-day orders, but nobody told me what 30-day orders meant. I had turned in my orders to the commanding officer. I assumed that it was his business to tell me what to do next, and he never told me to do anything. I happened to mention to somebody after two months that I was there on 30-day orders, and he said, "Well, what are you doing here?"

I said, "Waiting for somebody to tell me what to do next."

He said, "Well, you'd better tell the commander," so I went and told him. Then I was shipped off immediately to Washington.

Q: Was there any sense of disappointment in leaving?

Dr. Karpeles: Oh, no. I was happy to be going back. I still thought that I was likely to be working in Washington. After all, my family was there, and it was a good place to be. But I got back, and you had to have a badge to get into even these temporary buildings, so I went to apply for my badge. I knew enough to do that by this time. A guy shuffled through some papers and said, "You don't need a badge."

So I said, "I can't get into the building."

He said, "You don't need to get into the building. You're going to Pearl Harbor."
[Laughter]

Q: Had there been any kind of badge procedure up at Boston for getting into the Navy yard on a daily basis?

Dr. Karpeles: I don't remember it, but I think there must have been. A badge procedure is a pretty stupid business, in a way, because there are people that play games with the badges. Nobody ever picked anybody up playing games with the badges, unless somebody would put a photo of a monkey on his badge or something like that. You'd go right on through, so badges didn't mean a lot.

Q: Do you know if your background was ever checked to see if there was any precaution against sabotage or what have you?

Dr. Karpeles: I was told I had been given confidential clearance, and I took it for granted that there'd been a check. It may have been that somebody told me that there had been some questions asked about me. But I was stupid enough to think that if the Navy gave me confidential clearance, they knew what they were doing.

Q: And I think they probably would have been more apprehensive about foreign-born workers.

Dr. Karpeles: Well, I suppose, but I think our experience of recent years indicates that there's not much protection. But the truth was that most of the stuff that I was reading at the time--if not all of it--was classified "restricted." That meant the Navy wasn't sending the information to the newspapers for publication, but that's about all it meant. Anyhow, that was about the way we interpreted it.

Q: The classification of restricted was not as high as confidential.

Dr. Karpeles: No, not as high as confidential, and that's not as high as secret. And secret is not as high as top secret. I never got cleared above confidential, and yet I'm sure some kind of a check was made for that clearance. I thought at the time that the handling of classified material was remarkably careless. I heard it said that when the new information officer took over at Pearl Harbor and was presented with a list of classified material he was responsible for, he refused to sign it until it had been inventoried. When it was inventoried, they found they were 3,000 documents short in the confidential-and-up level. Security was a mess in that tour. I'm surprised if there were any secrets at all, because I worked in Honolulu Harbor for a while.

Q: When did you go out to Hawaii?

Dr. Karpeles: I went out to Hawaii in April 1942. I was very surprised when they flew me from Treasure Island out to Hawaii.[*] They blacked out the plane for landing. When I got out and saw the harbor, I was quite astonished to find all those hulks sitting on the bottom, because the news reports in the States had been that damage had been light. The Navy claimed publicly that everything but the Oklahoma, I think, was supposed to be back in service, which was pretty ridiculous.

I don't know who knew what, but after I'd been there a little while they assigned me to Honolulu Harbor, where there was a shuttle going on. There were ten ships--Liberty ships and other ships of comparable size--in each of four flotillas that went back and forth to San Francisco.[†] There was always one flotilla going, one flotilla coming, one flotilla in Honolulu Harbor, and one flotilla in San Francisco Harbor. They made a pretty regular shuttle. It was not so regular that you knew exactly when they were going out or coming in, but the harbormaster knew. They had antisubmarine gates or nets at the entrance to Honolulu Harbor. When they opened the nets, they were pretty antsy, because they didn't want a submarine coming in. So they'd get all the ships ready to go and the tugboats assembled to get them out. Then they'd open the submarine gates, and these ten ships would go zipping out in a period of 30 minutes or less.

---

[*] Treasure Island is a man-made island in San Francisco Bay, located between San Francisco and Oakland. It served as the site of a world's fair in 1939-40, then was converted for use as a Navy base during and after World War II.
[†] The Liberty ship was a mass-produced cargo ship designed by the U.S. Maritime Commission for use by the Allies. All told, American shipyards built 2,770 Liberties. The standard Liberty was 442 feet long, 57 feet in the beam, and had a light displacement of 3,337 tons. It had a cargo capacity of 10,920 deadweight tons.

On our ranging station we were supposed to check all the magnetic fields as the ships went out. We'd be sitting around doing nothing, and all of a sudden somebody said, "The ships are starting to move." We'd jump up and start trying to get ready for them and find out what ships they were, which you had to know. We tried to figure out the corrections for the coils and send them out by signal light to each ship before it was over the horizon, but it was too difficult.

Q: Did you have a cable laid under the harbor mouth or how did you measure the magnetic fields?

Dr. Karpeles: We had a line of coils spaced, as I recall, 30 feet apart all across the channel. They came up to flux meters that measured magnetic fields. The meters were in this shed right beside the channel where we worked. After a while, I started inquiring around: "Who plans the sailings?"

Somebody said, "Well, the captain of the yard does." So I went to see the gentleman, who was a commander in the Coast Guard, a nice guy. He said, "Yeah, I can see you've got a problem. What are we going to do about it?"

We had kept a log of the ships that went by, so I had recorded all the ships we had ever seen--perhaps 100 altogether. I put them in a typewritten list and assigned them numbers: one, two, three, four, right on down. I gave him a copy, and I kept a copy. He would call me over the open phone lines and call off a list of numbers. That would tell me the ships that were coming up, and it was a wonderful system as far as getting the information I needed and getting the information the ships needed to the ships. But with the kind of intelligence organization I imagine countries at war use, I imagine enemy agents would presumably have a way of tapping into the phone lines. If they detected these lists of numbers, it wouldn't be very long before they'd start associating them with the movements of the ships. I never thought about abandoning it, and the commander never did either, and we did that all the time I was down there. Nothing bad happened.

Q: Well, as far as that goes, somebody could sit there and watch what ships were going out.

Dr. Karpeles: Yes, but they had to watch in waters that they thought were pretty dangerous, and they could find out only after the ships had gone out. They'd like to know before the ships go out.

Q: Oh, I see. This was sometime in advance of the departure.

Dr. Karpeles: A couple of hours before the departure, the captain of the yard would let me know what to expect.

Q: So the degaussing equipment on board was to enhance whatever the deperming had done.

Dr. Karpeles: Yes. The deperming never really did its job, but assuming that it had, then the equipment on board was solely to take care of the induced field, which was substantial because of the mere fact of the ship existing in the earth's magnetic field. There were all different degrees of sophistication in the installations that went on different kinds of ships. A Liberty ship had one coil, and any kind of a warship had at least three coils. A minesweeper would have elaborate systems of coils on some occasions, trying to compensate for the magnetism in the propeller shaft--things like that. The transports were very carefully degaussed, but cargo ships not.

Q: Did you find as time went on that they needed smaller corrections?

Dr. Karpeles: Yes, because we all got better at our job as time went on. One of the interesting things was that as the ships came in and you would range them, they would signal us what their coil settings were. We would have on file what their coil settings were supposed to be, so we could check whether they were set right. Then we would have a record of the field that they demonstrated as they came in, and we would correct their instructions with a set of charts we'd give them--charts of the world. Whatever part of the world you're in, you're supposed to have this setting on your M coil. Settings on the F and Q coils you change with the heading, and we'd issue them a new set of charts.*

One of my little functions was to go aboard the ships and see the captain and give him his charts and be sure he understood them. Frequently the crews of the ships were not very welcoming of people who'd just come aboard and say, "I want to talk to the captain." So I went out and bought a nice briefcase. I was always in khakis, but I would come with this briefcase and had very little trouble getting to see the captain.

Q: Psychological.

Dr. Karpeles: Yes. If I had a little envelope full of papers I couldn't see him, but if I had a briefcase with papers in it, I could see him. If I didn't need to carry papers in the briefcase, I could carry my lunch in it, but I had to have something to carry. [Laughter]

Q: Did you get the idea that the masters of these ships were being provided intelligence on Japanese mine locations?

Dr. Karpeles: No. In the first place, most of the ships that I was seeing were only cruising back and forth to San Francisco. I don't think there were any Japanese mine locations, which was probably just as well.

Q: So this was really a case of being safe rather than sorry.

Dr. Karpeles: Yes, and, of course, any ship could be pulled off that run at any time and assigned anything else. Occasionally I would go aboard a ship that had been on the

---

* F and Q--forecastle and quarterdeck.

Murmansk run, and the response then was amazing.* I would approach the gangway watch and say, "I'm from the degaussing organization."

They'd say, "Yes, sir. Right this way, sir. The captain wants to see you, sir." The captain would meet me, offer me a cup of coffee, and say, "I want the engineering officer up here." Then we'd sit around the table and discuss the charts. The reason was that on the Murmansk run they were running into mines very regularly. What we hoped they didn't know--and I certainly never enlightened anybody--was that the reason that the ships that they saw sink on the Murmansk run sank so dramatically was that they were so well degaussed. They could pass a mine at 60 feet, and it wouldn't fire. So when it fired within 40 feet, the ship would go up in the air after the mine blew up. You could see the keel, and then she would break, fall, and sink. That left a lasting impression on the other people. They wanted the best degaussing they can get.

Q: Well, certainly your purpose was not to get the ships closer to the magnetic mines.

Dr. Karpeles: The purpose was to get them through. Nobody talked to me about military science and tactics, but I presume the assumption was that if a ship was sunk it didn't make a whole lot of difference whether it sunk in ten minutes or ten hours. They didn't want them sunk. A mine could sink an unprotected ship for sure at 200 feet. But if you could get the range necessary for an explosion down to 40 feet, you had increased the chances of the ship getting through by a factor of five or ten, and that was well worth the effort. If they didn't get through, they met an especially violent end. The same thing held true with the minesweepers. Minesweepers were degaussed down to a gnat's frazzle, but if they got too close to a mine, the effects would be devastating. It wouldn't be just a matter of sinking.

Q: For example, some of those steel-hulled minesweepers were lost in the Normandy invasion.

---

* As part of supplying war materials to the Soviet Union under the Lend-Lease program, some U.S. merchant ships had to steam to Murmansk in north Russia. The ships were susceptible to heave German attacks on that route.

Dr. Karpeles: Yes, big 220-foot jobs. The wood-hulled minesweepers were a lot better suited to the job. By the time of the Normandy invasion, they were in a lot of trouble with acoustic mines anyhow, which were much more of a problem.

Q: The steel-hulled ones had been built before the magnetic mine threat became known.

Dr. Karpeles: Yes, but we were able to put pretty good degaussing installations on them.

Q: How did the pace of work in Hawaii compare with what it had been in Boston?

Dr. Karpeles: More laid back, on the whole. Laid back isn't really the right word. It was more that we got to where we knew what we were doing, and we had the right equipment, we had enough people, and we were working seven days a week but eight hours a day, for the most part. We weren't worrying about overtime, but mostly we weren't working overtime.

Q: Was there any provision in your contract for overtime?

Dr. Karpeles: Not in that contract I was hired on. After I had been at Pearl Harbor for about a year, somebody decided that this was a lousy way to get personnel; they wanted everybody on Civil Service. We had a Commander Boyd at that time who was pretty good at getting along with people he had working for him.*

Q: Was he attached to the Navy yard at Pearl?

Dr. Karpeles: He was with the 14th Naval District, but there must have been some little tangles in the chain of command, connecting him to the Navy yard and the Bureau of

---

* Commander Thales S. Boyd, USN (Ret.).

Ordnance. In any event, he called each of us in individually and said, "We're under pressure to put you guys on Civil Service. How do you feel about that?"

We all said, "We like this arrangement." Under our contracts, there were no deductions from our paychecks. We worked seven days a week. I think I was up to $9.00 a day by this time, but if you worked for $7.00 or $9.00, or whatever it was, you would know what your paycheck was going to be--just multiply $7.00 by the number of days. It was an arrangement we liked. We didn't know about Civil Service, but we were pretty sure we didn't like it because it sounded complicated.

Q: Did you have an open-ended contract, or was there a finite term to it?

Dr. Karpeles: I don't recall that I ever had a piece of paper in my hand that was my contract. I was very trusting.

Q: And the money kept coming.

Dr. Karpeles: The money kept coming, and I don't remember any contract. I was told I was on a contract, and so Commander Boyd said, "Well, if we have to go on Civil Service, what grade do you want?" I figured out what grade I would have to be to make what I was making already, and then I asked for one grade higher. That was pretty much what everybody did, and we all got it.

Q: What grade did you come in at?

Dr. Karpeles: I am pretty sure it was a GS-7. At that time I think it paid $3,200 a year. My new salary was more than I'd been making, and it had annual leave in it. You didn't get your annual leave, but you got paid overtime for your annual leave. It had sick leave, whatever that was worth, but I was sick for only a couple days after that. We went on Civil Service, and it was fine once I got used to it.

Q: What were your living arrangements out there?

Dr. Karpeles: They varied. At first I was in a rooming house on Wilder Avenue, and then as I made friends we began to find rooming houses where we could live together. There was a clear dichotomy in that degaussing division between people who had been there on December 7, 1941, and people who came later. Even if you had come on December 9, you could never be one of the group that had been there on December 7. It was just different.

Q: Was there any condescension in manner or attitude from these men?

Dr. Karpeles: No, it was the same thing that you see in the Navy all the time. The guys who would sit around saying, "In the old Navy you couldn't have got away with this, that, or the other thing." It was all friendly enough.

A whole bunch of Japanese had been interned on December 8, and whole bunch of very desirable property had become suddenly available on December 8. So the guys who were there at the time had rented nice quarters on the shores of Pearl Harbor. Let's see, it was Pearl City, which was between East Loch and Middle Loch in the harbor. So they had these quarters, and there was personnel turnover, so that as the older guys left--old guys like 25--they would take in some of the newer people. In due course of time, we newer people were all that was left. We had this lovely mansion on the shores of the harbor that we rented for peanuts, really. That's where I lived for the last year or year and a half that I was at Pearl Harbor.

There came a time when somebody decided to organize a PT base at Pearl City and assigned an admiral to be the commander of the PT base.* We were adjacent to Pearl City, so an adjutant to the admiral dropped by one day and said, "How would you guys like to turn this place over to the admiral?"

At that time our household consisted of two jaygees and two civilians. The two jaygees said, "Yes, sir," and the two civilians said, "No way." [Laughter]

---

* PT--motor torpedo boat.

Well, the other civilian wasn't as hardheaded as I was. He knuckled under a little bit, and so that left me holding out. By that time a lieutenant commander was running this division. He called me in, and he said, "You're giving Admiral So-and-So and lot of trouble."

"I'm not giving him any trouble. I just want to live where I live."

He said, "Well, he wants that for his place."

I said, "That's too bad. I'm living there."

He said, "What's your draft status."

I said, "I'm deferred as a key man."

He said, "Well, how would you like to get drafted?"

I said, "I'm ready to get drafted any old time."

He said, "Oh. Well, look, what can we do to make you happy?"

I said, "Well, can you find me good quarters?"

"We can't find quarters like you're living in, but I can find you free quarters." So he put me up in a BOQ for the rest of the time I was at Pearl Harbor, and I got out of his hair.*

Q: Now, you mentioned the departure of these old timers--the men who were at Pearl Harbor on 7 December 1941. Did they join the Navy, or what happened to them?

Dr. Karpeles: Some of them were already in the Navy. Some of them were ensigns and jaygees at the time, and others did join. Some of the officers were already there as degaussing officers, and they were safe. But I knew some men who took commissions as ensigns in the line after they got there. The next thing they knew, they were deck officers on small ships.

I applied when this directive came through that said that the Navy desperately needed physicists to send to advance bases. At the time Congress had some law that no civilians could go west of Pearl Harbor. Instead, they wanted you to apply for a commission. So I trotted right down to the recruiting office and said, "We got this directive that says that you want to sign us guys up as commissioned officers. Here I am."

---

* BOQ--bachelor officers' quarters.

This two-stripe lieutenant whose name I don't know said, "Well, why do you want to be an officer in the Navy?"

"I don't want to be an officer in the Navy. I got this directive that says that this is what they need, and I'm prepared to do what they need."

Q: You were trying to be patriotic, as you had been.

Dr. Karpeles: I was trying to be patriotic, but I wasn't a damn bit interested in getting killed. And he said, "Well, it's considered an honor to be an officer in the United States Navy."

I said, "I'm sure it is, but I'm happy where I am."

He said, "I don't think you've got the right attitude." So, because I had the wrong attitude, I never got a commission, and I never got to be a deck officer on a destroyer. I'd have been a mess if I had been an officer.

Q: You probably would have had to take a pay cut too.

Dr. Karpeles: Well, perhaps or perhaps not, but I wasn't really thinking about that aspect of it. You couldn't spend money in Honolulu; it was practically impossible. Unless you were looking for a quick lay or something, there was nothing you could do. So I was putting away $1,000 a year out of my income. What I was doing was saving up to go to medical school, but I didn't know that at the time. That's just where the money ultimately went. But I wasn't thinking about money.

Q: What do you remember of hearing of the various events of the war while you were there in Hawaii, such as the Battle of Midway and on after that?

Dr. Karpeles: Oh, we got information mostly from the newspapers. For sleeping comfortably at night, the Battle of Midway was a turning point.* Up to that time, Pearl Harbor was defended largely by weapons that had been salvaged off the Arizona.† The story was that guys that were willing to get the most blisters got the guns, because they went aboard her as soon as she began to cool down. If they could stand the heat to unbolt a gun and take it off the ship, they'd unbolt it and take it off the ship and then they had a gun. Nobody owned them. If anybody owned them, they didn't admit it.

Q: I think there may have been a little folklore in that.

Dr. Karpeles: Well, maybe so.

Q: Some of the 14-inch guns were later used in shore batteries on Oahu.

Dr. Karpeles: Oh, I'm not talking about 14 inches. I'm talking about .50-caliber machine guns. The big guns, I'm sure, were a different matter. But there was very little defense. There was a coil of barbed wire along Waikiki Beach which a few 5-inch shells would have just blown to pieces.

Q: Did you feel any apprehension when you first got there?

---

* From 4 to 6 June 1942, U.S. and Japanese naval forces fought a battle northwest of Midway Island in the Pacific. After Japanese bombers had struck the island, carrier-based U.S. dive-bombers attacked and sank the Japanese carriers Hiryu, Soryu, Kaga, and Akagi and the cruiser Mikuma. U.S. ships lost were the carrier Yorktown (CV-5) and the destroyer Hammann (DD-412). The battle was both a tactical and strategic victory for U.S. forces.

† The battleship Arizona (BB-39), commissioned in 1916, was heavily damaged on 7 December 1941 when a Japanese high-level bomber hit her with an armor-piercing projectile converted to a bomb. Her forward magazines exploded as a result, leading to a fire that burned for a few days afterward. Of the ship's crew of 1,514 at the time of the attack, 1,177 were killed.

Dr. Karpeles: Oh, sure. I was still this hero. My brother-in-law was in the National Guard, so he'd been called up early. But before he want away, he heard I was going out to Pearl Harbor. He was a gun buff and turned over a pistol to me. So I went out there with a .45-caliber pistol prepared to do or die.

They had a civilian defense corps; it was a bunch of old men and a few guys like me. We drilled on some park land or something with Krag 30-30 rifles. We had an idea that we might be going to have to use this kind of foolishness, and maybe we were going to be living in the hills back of Honolulu and that kind of thing. How much of it was romanticism and how much of it was a real possibility, we didn't know and I don't know yet. But we knew after Midway that that probably wasn't going to happen. Up to that time we read all about Wake Island and Bataan and that sort of thing.* There wasn't any good reason to know it wasn't going to happen on Oahu, so Midway was a tremendous relief.

Q: Did the nature of your job change any? Did you get involved with the combatant ships in addition to these Liberty ships at any time.

Dr. Karpeles: Yes, the nature of my job changed at least twice. I went out there to Pearl Harbor, and we were working on all kinds of warships. Then I was transferred to Honolulu Harbor, and we were working entirely on cargo vessels and some transports. I was later called back to Pearl Harbor, because they wanted somebody to take care of acoustic mine defense. My commanding officer called me up one day and said, "What do you know about acoustics?"

I said, "I had a course in acoustics once."

He said, "What do you know about electronics?"

I said, "I had a course in electronics once."

He said, "Well, we're going to make you our new acoustics expert. Don't worry about it, because Campbell [a jaygee] can break you in on this stuff before he goes west."

---

* The Japanese captured Wake Island in December 1941 and the Bataan Peninsula in the Philippines in the spring of 1942.

So I met Campbell. He took me out and showed me the equipment, and the next day he left. I had all this equipment I knew nothing about. It didn't even occur to me to requisition a book. I just went downtown, took some money out of my pocket, and bought a textbook on electronics. Then I sat at my desk for about two weeks and studied the book on electronics, got the hang of it, and started running this acoustic range.

Q: Where was it geographically?

Dr. Karpeles: The acoustic range was geographically Waipio Point, if that means anything to you. So mostly we were doing two different things. We were recording the sounds of our own ships and analyzing them to find what frequency bands they fell in. We sent that information back to Washington to do with whatever they did with it. I never knew. As far as I was concerned, recording it, calibrating the recording equipment, analyzing the records, and sending back the analysis ended my contact.

Then they started developing new types of acoustic mines and involved me in that. It was kind of weird, because anything connected with these new mines was secret, and I wasn't cleared for secret. My commanding officer would take out all these papers and turn them over to me, and I would work with them. The equipment wasn't much good, but I was getting pretty smart by then, so I kept modifying the equipment. After a year it didn't look anything like the instruction books.

Finally came my orders to go back to the States. I went to the commander, and I said, "What are we going to do about all this equipment?"

He said, "Just give me back all the books that I have loaned you, and we'll be fine."

I said, "Well, the books aren't worth anything. Everything has been completely rewired. It doesn't look anything like the books."

He said, "Well, you'll have to get busy and write us some new manuals."

I said, "Okay, but this stuff's all secret."

He said, "Okay, you can write it."

I said, "I can't sign it."

He says, "You write it. I'll sign it." So I drew up a new set of instruction manuals for all this equipment, and it involved a lot of wiring diagrams. I drew up the wiring diagrams and marked them all secret all over the place, just like I knew what I was doing. Then I took them over to the ozalid room, which was the kind of duplication we had then, and I said, "I need three copies of each of these."

The guy who was there said, "Okay." He started running them through the ozalid machine, and they came out. Sometimes he would say, "That's not a very good copy," and threw it in the trash. He didn't know me. I was just somebody with a badge who came in and said he wanted these things duplicated.

Finally, he got me my three copies, and I said, "What do you do with that trash?"

"I don't know. It's trash."

I said, "You see this stuff's marked secret?"

He said, "What's that mean?"

I said, "Would you take those things out of the trash and give them to me, and I'll see that they're destroyed." So he took them out of the trash and gave them to me. I took them back to the commander and said, "Here are the copies, and here's the trash that was associated with it." So he signed off all those instruction books that I wrote.

Q: Where was the deperming facility at Pearl Harbor?

Dr. Karpeles: Beckoning Point, which was half an hour by boat from Ten-Ten Dock in the Navy yard. It was about 15 minutes by boat from Pearl City, where seven of us degaussers lived. The Navy used to ferry us to work every day.

Q: And its capability was much more, you said, than you'd had back in Boston.

Dr. Karpeles: Oh, yes, yes. For one thing, they had a coil around the whole facility on the bottom of the harbor. They could set that coil to simulate the magnetic field anywhere on earth. So that if the ship was going to the Marianas they could set the coil for the Marianas and deperm the ship for the Marianas. Even if she wasn't depermed where she sat, she would be depermed where she was going. Yes, that was a much more sophisticated installation.

Q: When was it that the commander asked you to write these instruction manuals?

Dr. Karpeles: Just prior to my departure, which was about February 1945. They sent me to San Diego, and I was there a few months before I was drafted in May.

Q: So you were out in Hawaii for about three years.

Dr. Karpeles: Almost three years, and it was certainly exciting. We saw a lot of battle damage there.

Q: Any that you remember specifically?

Dr. Karpeles: What I remember most clearly is that the Washington rammed the Indiana.[*] As I heard the story, it was some innocent maneuver that the Indiana got the signal for the fleet to turn and the Washington didn't get it. So the Indiana turned across her bow, and you could see what had happened. The Washington's bow had evidently been in a trough when she hit the Indiana. The bow had been rising, so that the bow of the Washington was turned down, oh, about an 80-degree angle, right in front of the forward turrets. The torpedo blister of the Indiana was torn off from midships to stern with Bofors guns hanging out over the water. The 16-inchers were hanging out over the water on the Washington. It was a mess.

Q: Did you get opportunities for relaxation?

---

[*] The collision was on the night of 1 February 1944. The Washington (BB-56) arrived at Pearl Harbor on 18 February to have a temporary bow fitted before she steamed to the West Coast for permanent repairs.

Dr. Karpeles: When I was in Honolulu, we used to go to the Waikiki Theater every Sunday. They had a beautiful theater with all reserved seats. We bought our seats one week for the show the next week without even asking what the show was going to be. We had to be home before dark, so we'd go in the afternoon down to the theater and catch a movie and go home. The Army had taken over the Punahou School in Honolulu, and our badges would get us in there. They showed movies in the open air on the tennis courts or something for the enlisted men there, and we were allowed to go there. I don't know. You adapt to what you have, and we had plenty compared to what a lot of people had. They had guys that could play a guitar, and so we'd sit around with the guitar and sing. We played poker sometimes.

Then some of the fellows had a mansion just below Diamond Head. They had a very fine hi-fi system, and we'd go visit them and drink a little and listen to the hi-fi.* They had a tremendous glass patio that looked out over the ocean. There was no way they could black it out, so they had the back half of the house blacked out, and you had to be very careful going from the front half to the back half to maintain the blackout. But you could sit there and watch the phosphorescence of the ocean and listen to this fine music. I remember I had a good time at Pearl Harbor.

Q: Who was the group that you associated with?

Dr. Karpeles: It was mostly physicists and junior officers from the degaussing division.

Q: How many physicists would have gathered by, let's say, the midpoint in the war--'43, '44?

Dr. Karpeles: A dozen.

Q: Still a pretty exclusive group.

---

* Hi-fi, short for high fidelity, was the latest in record players at the time.

Dr. Karpeles: Yes, but we also had about the same number of junior officers. We had different stations around. Every station had to have a commanding officer, and some of them have to have an executive officer as well. There was reasonably good rapport between the officers and the civilians. Every once in a while, somebody would feel it necessary to explain to the civilians that they were a lower order of humanity, but nobody was much impressed with it when it happened.

Q: I gather there came a time when you felt much more of a sense of confidence that you'd had back in Boston.

Dr. Karpeles: Oh, yes. I got to where I really knew what I was doing. I knew a lot of stuff that the people who'd sent me out from Washington didn't know. They sent a Ph.D. physicist out at one point to check on my work. He saw what I was doing and said, "This is all wrong. This isn't the way you're supposed to do it."

I said, "Well, I started out doing it the way you're supposed to do it, but this is the way it works." He was pretty unhappy. He spent some months taking notes and checking over everything I'd done, and he finally came to the conclusion that I was right. I had developed some better ways of doing things, and so he went away happy.

Q: As time went on, did you write any reports on what you were doing?

Dr. Karpeles: No, except these things that I never signed. The data that I collected on acoustic equipment I think was forwarded by the commander of the division. I didn't have anything to do with it. I'd just take in the charts.

Q: Well, I mentioned earlier the business of intelligence reports on Japanese mining. That wouldn't have as much application on a voyage to San Francisco. What about as the ships were moving farther west?

Dr. Karpeles: There was a lot of application. I have no idea how many mines actually damaged American ships, but there certainly were a lot of mined waters out there.

Q: Did you get reports on what the mined waters were?

Dr. Karpeles: Oh, no. We had no idea of that. Somebody must have known, but we sure didn't. We were just told to degauss this ship for such-and-such a place and presume that there were mines there. Need-to-know things sort of applied. People didn't tell you stuff you didn't need to know, and you didn't ask stuff you didn't need to know. All kinds of rumors ran around, and we enjoyed the rumors, but we had a pretty good idea what stock to take in them.

Q: What sorts of rumors were they?

Dr. Karpeles: I mentioned the thing about people who put monkey faces on their badges and got around fine on them.

There was a also story about dry dock four at the Navy yard. They were building the Iowa-class battleships and got them commissioned.* So these ships had to have a forward dry dock that could accommodate them. Pearl Harbor didn't have any, so we--we, meaning this camaraderie of the Navy yard--were building a big dry dock to accommodate these Iowa-class ships. I think they probably started excavating for the dry dock about the same time they laid the keels of the ships, and the two jobs took about the same length of time.

The story was that some hotshot intelligence officer made himself a fake badge, entered the Navy yard carrying a suitcase, and asked a number of different Marine guards the way to the number-four dry dock. They all gave him good directions. He got to number-four dry dock, and he set this suitcase down outside the door of the deck house that

---

* The four ships of the Iowa (BB-61) class were commissioned between February 1943 and June 1944.

was going to do the pumping for the dry dock. He left it there, came back four days later, and the suitcase was still sitting there. Nobody had asked him, "What's in your suitcase? Where are you going? What do you need to know about number-four dry dock?" It was just weird.

Q: Did things tighten up at all after that?

Dr. Karpeles: I don't know. It may be an apocryphal story. I never knew it personally. I never knew that thing about the 3,000 missing documents personally. It was one of the rumors. But things never seemed tight.

I certainly knew about my arrangement for ranging ships out of Honolulu Harbor, and that wasn't tight. Outside Honolulu Harbor we had a magnetic submarine detector. It was very sophisticated for its time and very effective. We could detect a small boat with a steel hull--I mean, we're talking about a boat the size of an LCVP--going across this submarine detection would set it off.[*] We maintained a watch 24 hours a day on it there in Honolulu Harbor for, oh, a good year and got to know the kind of signatures every kind of ship made.

One fine day a ship registered on our equipment, but there was no ship. Our instructions were to call the captain of the yard and tell him if we ever detected a submarine. So I called and said, "This is Leo Karpeles down at the degaussing station. You know me. We've got a submarine outside the submarine gates.

He said, "No, you don't."

I said, "Yes, we do. What makes you say we don't?"

He said, "I can see. I'm up in Aloha Tower.[†] I can see out there. There's no submarine."

I said, "The submarine is under the water. It's there."

He said, "How can you know? If it's under the water, how do you know it's there?"

---

[*] LCVP--landing craft, vehicle, personnel, which was 36 feet long.
[†] Aloha Tower is a major landmark in Honolulu Harbor. It is situated near the passenger ship terminal.

"Well, we've got this magnetic loop out there."

"How does it work?"

"It doesn't matter how it works. There's a submarine out there."

So about an hour and a half later a subchaser went out. By then there wasn't any submarine, and this officer said, "See, I told you there wasn't any submarine." We knew it. The signature was gone, but it had been there. So some Japanese submarine once upon a time did come and lurk outside Honolulu harbor for a little while.

That kind of thing sort of typifies my experience with the Navy in dealing with any unusual situation. I think probably the Navy has instructions to take three battleships to such and such a location and unload their entire 16-inch armament into that island. They can do that just fine, but they have problems with something out of the ordinary.

Q: Do you remember the LST explosion at the ammunition depot?[*]

Dr. Karpeles: Oh, yes. Yes, indeed. I guess it started in the afternoon. I was still at the office. I forget whom I called. I guess I first called my own commander and said, "Do we have any responsibility for this?" and he said he didn't know.

I called somebody else, and he said, "No, we don't have any responsibility. Forget it." And I was happy, because I could see it from my place, and it was big stuff. I didn't want any responsibility, so I went back out to Pearl City my regular time, and that thing kept on blowing until something like midnight. In my innocence or ignorance, I thought the whole damn West Loch had blown up. I'd been in West Loch, and I knew what was up there. With the amount of fireworks we were seeing, it was hard to imagine that it wasn't everything that was up there. Half a dozen of these LSTs were moored abreast. They were all loaded with ammunition, and fire broke out in one of them and spread to the whole bunch of them.

---

[*] On 21 May 1944, a tank landing ship exploded and caught fire while loading mortar ammunition at West Loch in Pearl Harbor. All told, six LSTs and three LCTs were lost. The casualties were 163 dead and 396 injured. See Howard E. Shuman, "The Other Pearl Harbor Disaster," Naval History, Summer 1988, pages 32-36.

The Terror was up there, fully loaded with mines.* Every signal light in the yard, including ours, was trained on that ship, and they were all sending one signal: "Go to sea. Go to sea. Go to sea." And that's exactly what the Terror did. I understand they cut the lines with a fire axes and just took off. They had a little steam up, and they left. If that ship had blown, it would have been a big display.

Q: What was the procedure by which you finally got drafted and went into the service?

Dr. Karpeles: Well, all the time I was at Pearl Harbor I never saw any communication from my draft board. At some point, for some thoroughly unrelated reason, I went over to the records building. They had a building that was supposed to be bombproof. That's where the records were kept, and I asked to see my personnel record about something. They gave it to me, and as I flipped through it, I found that a tango had been going on all the time I had been at Pearl Harbor.

The draft board would classify me 1-A and mail this classification to me, but it never got to me. It just went to this deferment office at Pearl Harbor, and they would write back and appeal the classification. The appeal of the classification would come back rejected, and then they would write back and say, "Mr. Karpeles is classified as a key man, because a physicist is a key man." They were allowed 500 key men for the whole Navy, and basically they were keeping about 2,000 or 3,000 men on this key-man roster by juggling it. If the draft was really hot on somebody's neck, he was a key man. As soon as the fire died down, somebody else could use that position.

So, again, because of this concept of patriotism or whatever it was, I said, "This isn't right. I am being deferred by finagling such as I would never indulge in." I wrote the commander of my division and said, "I want to be responsible for my own negotiations with selective service."

He said, "You can't do that. Nobody at the Navy yard does that. It's all handed by the selective service office we've got set up."

---

* The USS Terror (CM-5) was a large minelayer.

I said, "Well, I've been here almost three years now, and I want to go stateside." So he arranged for me to go stateside. I was going to San Diego, so I sent a communication to the commander of the degaussing unit there. I said that the reason I was coming stateside was that I wanted to have control of my own selective service status, and he said okay. V-E Day had passed during this time, so that the draft board was much hotter to pull in people who had been deferred in the Pacific--deferred anywhere--than they had been.[*] And so we got there with this understanding that I would be in control of my own draft status. It wasn't very long before I got "Greetings."

I went to the commander, and I said, "I've got orders to report to my draft station, the station in Washington."

He said, "Well, I'll tell you what you do. You get them to transfer it to San Diego as being a hardship for you to have to go to Washington, and meanwhile we'll take care of it."

I said, "That's just not what I want to do on two counts. One, I don't want to be a draft dodger. I've never thought of myself as a draft dodger, and I'm not about to cooperate in a draft-dodging operation now. That's number one. Number two is if I get drafted out here, there's no telling when I'll ever see my family again, and I'd rather be drafted in Washington, where at least I'll get a home visit out of the whole thing." He was pretty pissed.

The selective service was paying my fare back to Washington, but when I got back to Washington I reported to the office I was told to report to, and they said, "You've been reclassified. We can't induct you."

I said, "I've got this paper here. It says to report for induction."

"Well, you'll have to take that up with PR-8D over at the Navy building."

So I went over there and I said, "What's this all about?"

They said, "Well, your commanding officer out in San Diego says you're a key man and that you're not draftable."

I said, "Well, I got orders to report, and I've reported."

---

[*] V-E Day--Victory in Europe Day, 8 May 1945, when the German surrender was ratified in Berlin.

He said, "Well, you've got orders now to go back to San Diego."

I said, "Okay, you cut the orders and give me a ticket, and I'll go back to San Diego."

He said, "You came here in defiance of your commanding officer's orders. If you want to go back to San Diego, you can pay your own way."

I said, "I don't want to go back to San Diego. If you want me back in San Diego, you're going to have to send me back."

"We're not going to send you back."

I said, "Okay, I live at 3549 16th Street. You can send my paychecks there." [Laughter] One paycheck went to 3549 16th Street before I got drafted. In the meantime, I went and took the exam for ET, because I figured if I was going to get drafted I'd rather be in the Navy than the Army.* So I passed the exam for ET, and I went to ET school.

Q: Did you have a choice in the induction, which service?

Dr. Karpeles: No. If I'd simply been inducted, I would almost surely have gone into the Army. But there was some kind a bulletin out that the Navy was examining people who thought they might qualify for electronics technician school. So I thought that any way I could get into the Navy was better than going in the Army. So I went up and took this examination. It was all physics, and it was an easy exam to pass. The next thing I was in boot camp; then I was in ET school.

Q: At that point there were no voluntary enlistments, so you had to be drafted to get in.

Dr. Karpeles: If that's so, I didn't know it. I was not going to go and volunteer, because I thought I was more useful as a physicist than I was as gun fodder. But at the same time I wasn't going to avoid the draft. I had the feeling that in general in the Navy you've got a bunk to sleep in. If your luck is bad and the ship sinks, you're dead, but the rest of the time

---

* ET--electronics technician, a Navy enlisted rating.

you've got a bunk to sleep in. In the Army you've got mud to sleep in, and you can spend any amount of time crawling around in the mud, and I'd thought I'd rather be in the Navy.

Q: Where did you go to boot camp?

Dr. Karpeles: Great Lakes.* I was lucky. I was lucky everywhere I went. The chief boatswain's mate that commanded the company I was put into was one great guy. He lined us all up, and he said, "We've got this foolishness about roosters. You'll find a lot of the guys are crazy to get roosters. You know, you've got ten weeks here. You've got to learn how to survive in a war, and I don't want you wasting your time getting a rooster. So you get this place cleaned enough that I don't get in trouble with the inspecting officer, and don't you worry about a rooster."

A rooster was a flag with a red rooster on it. It was awarded weekly, I think, to the company that had the best record--presumably the fewest black marks--on the Friday captain's inspection. I never wondered whether this was the practice throughout Great Lakes or just in some divisions of the boot camp. I always assumed there was only one rooster for the whole camp. So we all decided to bust our asses and get a rooster, and we did. It was just because we thought it would stand to his credit, and we liked him. He was a good Joe.

So I finished boot camp, no problem. They took me in as a seaman first class because of being in ET school. As a seaman first I was sent to Theodore Hertzel School in Chicago, where somebody started trying to teach me how to use a slide rule. I had been doing the most elaborate gymnastics with a slide rule for analysis of magnetic fields for years, and this guy said, "Now, you pull the sliding bar out until the one on the C scale on the sliding bar is over the two on the D scale, and then you take that little glass thing and slide that along and so forth." So I did it all. He came around and he checked that everybody was doing it right. After the class was over, I went up to him and I said, "I've

---

* Naval Training Station, Great Lakes, Illinois. Karpeles began his recruit training on 26 May 1945.

been using a slide rule for years, and I'm really quite good at it. I wonder if there's anything more useful you can have me do than sit here learning to multiply 2 by 2."

He said, "Are you a wise guy? Wise guy, you just do what everybody else does, and we'll tell you when you do something else." Okay, so I learned to use a slide rule. I never learned how to use it right there, but I knew how to use it, so that was all right. A lot of other stuff I learned that I already knew.

I guess it was while I was in Chicago that V-J Day came.[*] First the A-bomb came along and V-J Day not very long afterwards.[†] Nobody had any doubt after the A-bomb that the war was over. So they sent me to Biloxi, Mississippi, for my secondary training in this ET program, which was an 11-month program. Shortly after I got to Biloxi they closed the school, but they kept us there. Then, after about a week, they reopened the school, and about a week later they closed the school again. In a short period of time they said they were opening the school again, but people who would rather go to sea could drop out.

Well, a lot of guys were having a lot of trouble in the course, and I was bored with the course. So all the guys who were having trouble--and I--asked for sea duty. The reason was that it was worth a quarter of a point.[‡] It wasn't so much a matter of being bored. Everybody was after discharge points, and there was a quarter of a point extra for sea duty, so I was sent aboard the Alabama in San Francisco.[§]

Q: This was probably right around Navy Day then, wasn't it? She'd come back from the Far East.

---

[*] V-J Day--Victory over Japan Day, marking the end of the war in the Pacific on 15 August 1945.
[†] In the first combat use of atomic bombs, U.S. B-29 bombers hit Hiroshima, on the island of Honshu, on 6 August 1945 and Nagasaki, on Kyushu, on 9 August.
[‡] For the demobilization of the U.S. armed forces after World War II, the services had a point system to determine individual priorities for leaving the service. Points were awarded for length of service, overseas service, battle stars, decorations, and dependent children. Those with the highest number of points were the earliest discharged.
[§] The USS Alabama (BB-60) was commissioned 16 August 1942. She had a full-load displacement of 42,782 tons, was 680 feet long, had a beam of 108 feet, 2 inches, and a draft of 36 feet, 4 inches. Her top speed was 27.5 knots. The ship had nine 16-inch guns and 20 5-inch/38 dual-purpose guns.

Dr. Karpeles: She'd come back from the Far East. I don't know when she came back.* I think we were in the first draft of new men to go aboard after her return. There were 200 of us. We were all assigned to one or another menial duty. When I went aboard, they said, "What are you interested in?"

I said, "I'm interested in electronics."

They said, "Well, you should have stayed in ET school."

I said, "Yeah, but I didn't want to stay in ET school."

"What's your next best interest?"

"Well, how about electrical division?"

"Okay, you can be an electrician." So they sent me to the electrical division, and a warrant officer took me around to see the facilities of the electrical division on the Alabama. We came into the IC room, and two officers were bent over a table, going over a list of the new draftees.† One of them said, "This man here, I know this guy named Karpeles. I worked with him. You can't send him to the galley. I've got another job for him." He was the commanding officer at Beckoning Point when I was out there, and I never liked him. He never liked me. But he knew I could do something better than cook, and so he assigned me to take care of interior communications circuits, along with a lot of other people.

Rapidly they began discharging all the old-timers and bringing aboard new drafts. So it wasn't very long before there were very few of the people that really understood the interior communications that were aboard. I did understand them. I tried to be cagey, but I knew what I was doing. I would drop a word from time to time, "I think I can fix this, but it looks to me like it's a petty officer's type of job. Doesn't look like a seaman's job to me."

They'd say, "Well, you fix it." I'd fix it. Next thing that came up, I'd give them the same spiel but trying not to be pushy.

Q: They weren't getting the hint.

---

* The Alabama reached San Francisco on 15 October 1945, and on Navy Day, 27 October, she hosted 9,000 visitors.
† IC--interior communications.

Dr. Karpeles: Eventually they got the hint. I got the word that I was to report for third class petty officer exam, third class electrician's mate. When I was at Waipio Point, I had coached several of the seamen to take this exam. They were all finding the instruction book difficult, so I would go through it with them--problems about streetcars running on tracks and drawing so much current and so many volts, how many watts and things like that. So I knew all this stuff, and I could do it in my sleep. A bunch of us were taking this exam, and there was a warrant officer who was supervising, and he kept hovering behind me and making little humming noises. Every time I'd make a mark on the paper, "Uh-hmm, uh-hmm, uh-hmm, uh-hmm." At one point I started to make a mark, and he said, "Unh-unh, unh-unh."

I said, "Mr. Brooks, please don't worry. I'll be all right." [Laughter] So I made third class petty officer, which had the advantage that I was off most work details, and I didn't have to empty trash cans or sweep down--that sort of thing. I was in gravy. I was very good for what they wanted done. The standard technique for repairing electronic equipment in the interior communications organization was to put the defective equipment on a bench and start pulling out parts and replacing them out of the parts box and trying it out. When it finally worked, you took all the parts you'd pulled out, threw them over the side, and said, "There, it's fixed." They just weren't used to a guy that would get out the instruction book and read the instructions and say, "The trouble must be in this component, so let's replace it." I'd replace a component, and the thing worked.

Q: Did they have test equipment at that point?

Dr. Karpeles: Oh, yes, we were very well equipped, but nobody knew what he was doing. We had a telephone technician who really knew what he was doing, because he was a Bell Telephone guy before he ever came aboard. He introduced me to the automatic telephones, which I thought were just miraculous. I couldn't get over just watching those damn little switches switch, and so I learned that stuff. Spent my time on watch with a big thick book on the automatic telephones, because there wasn't anything else to do.

Q: Now, automatic in what sense? That you dial a number and it rings at the other end?

Dr. Karpeles: Yes, the dial system. It was a system with line finders and connecters, all stepping switches--nothing electronic in it at all. Not a vacuum tube or a transistor anywhere but very clever electromagnetic devices.

One problem in that ship was that we had fire alarms that were undependable. One of my jobs was taking care of them, and I took care of them as best I could. Everybody knew they were undependable. But we still had them, and we had instructions how to deal with fire alarms. So one fine day there was a fire alarm. I was on watch in the IC room, where there was nothing but a bell. My instructions were to call damage control and to call the officer of the deck. So I called the officer of the deck and said, "I'm in the IC room, and we've got a fire alarm."

He said, "Where's the fire?"

I said, "I don't know. All I've got is an alarm that says we've got a fire in some critical area of the ship."

He said, "What's the use of that if you don't know where the fire is?"

I said, "Well, they know that in damage control. I'm calling damage control next."

He said, "Okay, call damage control and call me right back."

So I called damage control, and I said, "Are you getting this fire alarm?"

He said, "What fire alarm?"

I said, "Isn't there a bell ringing in there?"

"Yeah. Is that a fire alarm?"

"Yes, that's a fire alarm."

"Well, what am I supposed to do?"

"I don't know what you're supposed to do, but I know what I'm supposed to do and I'm doing it."

So I called back to the officer of the deck, and I said, "The guy up in damage control doesn't know how to read the fire alarm system. I'm on duty here. Do you want to relieve me of duty so I can go up there and see?"

He says, "Yes, you're relieved. Go on up and see." It wasn't very far, so I went to damage control, which had a big panel full of lights. It said one of the powder magazines was registering a fire. Damage control had a lot of valves for the magazines, so they could flood any one of them.

I called the officer of the deck, and I said, "It's in such and such an ammunition compartment. Do you want me to flood it?"

"Hell, no, don't flood it. I'll be right down." He came down with the damage control officer, and they stared at the board and said, "How do we know there's a fire there?"

"We don't. It's probably a false alarm because the damn thing gives false alarms, but it says there's a fire there."

"Well, we can't flood that compartment if we don't know whether there's a fire or not. Send somebody down there."

It took half an hour. The guy who went down found the magazine locked with a padlock. Then he came back and reported that the captain had the key to the magazine. Then he was sent up to the captain's quarters. The Marine sentry outside the captain's quarters didn't want to let him in, but he finally got past the Marine sentry. The captain gave him the key, he went down and unlocked the magazine, found out there wasn't any fire. Well, any fool knew there wasn't any fire, because the ship was still intact. [Laughter] But this seemed to me to be the way things were going. Of course, this was after decommissioning was beginning. So this wasn't the crew that had taken the ship into battle. It's very possible that in those days they would have handled the whole thing much better. But it was pretty shocking.

Q: Your duty as an enlisted man in the Alabama was obviously a step down from the BOQ and the other palatial things you'd enjoyed in Hawaii. How did you adjust to the change?

Dr. Karpeles: Fine. I think I've always been adjustable. There were one or two of the crew I was associated with that I had trouble getting along with. It was not to the point of violence or threatened violence or anything of that kind, but just I wished the hell they'd stay out of my way and I could stay out of their way.

Also, there was a guy aboard who wanted to save my soul. My problem with him was he had to save everybody's soul, and I was the only guy who would talk to him. So he was after my soul constantly. That was a bit of a problem but very easy to take care of. The big thing was that I still under this electrical officer who knew me.

Q: What was his name?

Dr. Karpeles: Lieutenant Oberhausen. He was a snotty little bastard with a Hitler mustache. But it was sort of a thing going. If I asked for liberty, he wouldn't say, "When were you ashore last?" He would say, "How are the circuits working?" If I said they were working, they better damn sight be working. If I said they were, he'd say, "You can go on liberty." Because in the interior communications system I was probably the guy that best understood the whole setup except the sound-powered phones. I wasn't very hot on sound-powered phones. But mostly I knew what was going on in that setup.

Q: What do you remember about the messing and berthing arrangements in the Alabama?

Dr. Karpeles: As I recall, there were two mess calls, so that there was always somebody to relieve a watch and somebody to go to eat. There was, of course, a wardroom way off in officer country. I occasionally repaired a telephone in officer country, but I always felt like I was made in Japan or Germany or something. It wasn't where I belonged. And there was a chiefs' mess. I don't recall whether or not there was a petty officers' mess, which I had qualified for after I got my one stripe. I believe that mess hall must have been arranged around the barbette of a gun turret, because I recall it as having a big circular column right down through it.

Q: And you probably slept in bunks that were three or four tiers high.

Dr. Karpeles: Slept in bunks that were three or four tiers high until I got smarter and found that there was a space in the after gyro room. There were two gyros. I think one of them was in damage control, if I'm not mistaken. That was the one that the ship ordinarily conned by.* But there was a backup gyro, which was always running when we were at sea; that was down on the sixth level, somewhere in the forepeak of the ship. There was a moderate amount of space around that gyro, and nobody ever went down there but me.

I got hold of a sleeping pad and took it down. It was on a 4-inch armor deck. So I put my 2-inch pad on a 4-inch armor deck and slept like a baby. If the gyro was running, I could sleep; if the gyro was off, I could sleep. But if the gyro went off while I was sleeping, I'd wake up. But that's where I slept, because there would be our wakeup call, there would be a mess call, and there would be a muster call. I had to make the muster call, and I wanted to make the mess call, but I wasn't much interested it making the wakeup call. Down there I didn't have to, and furthermore when I had nothing to do I might disappear in the middle of the day. I'd go down there and catch a nap. One day I was down there catching a nap and Mr. Brooks, the warrant electrician, came through there with a flashlight. He stumbled over me and said, "Oh, excuse me." Then he went on and did whatever he did and never said another word about it. [Laughter]

Q: What were the ship's operations during that period after the war?

Dr. Karpeles: I went aboard in San Francisco. Then the ship went down to Long Beach and spent a long time there.† I think by that time we were starting the mothballing operation, and they shipped us up to Puget Sound for decommissioning. I went below decks while we were making kind of a stormy passage up to San Francisco. I got sick as a dog, then came above decks when we dropped anchor in Puget Sound. But San Francisco's

---

* The individual with the conn--normally an officer--directs the ship's movements in course and speed.
† After the Navy Day celebration in San Francisco, the <u>Alabama</u> left for Long Beach on 29 October. She remained there until 27 February 1946, when he left to go to Puget Sound Naval Shipyard, Bremerton, Washington, for inactivation overhaul.

a nice place; it's brown, and Puget Sound is green. I came up and looked around, the green hills coming right down to the water. "Man," I said, "this is my kind of country." So after I was discharged, I went back there and lived there a long time.

Q: Did you get the feeling during these West Coast operations that the ship was just going through the motions?

Dr. Karpeles: Yes. Nobody ever told me what was going on, but there wasn't anything to do.

I don't feel like I spent a lot of time in San Francisco on either of my tours. That's where I went aboard her, and we stopped there for a while going north. But we were in Long Beach for a couple of months. Before I joined the Navy, when I was in San Diego, I had started going to church. I'd never been a churchgoer, but I started going to the Unitarian Church in San Diego, and I went to the Unitarian Church in Long Beach long enough to get acquainted there, so it must have been a couple of months. Then it was back up to San Francisco and up to Puget Sound.

We were at Puget Sound long enough for me to fall in love. I met a girl at the church. I suppose we were there five months or so till I was discharged in August. By the time I was discharged I'd made up my mind that as soon as I was out I was coming back. Actually I didn't quite do it that way, but I went back the next summer. She and I got engaged, and later she and I got disengaged. But there was a gang I fell in with that were church people.

Q: Did you have a role in the inactivation while the ship was at Bremerton.

Dr. Karpeles: Yes, I scraped paint and painted. That's about all I remember. They mothballed the guns by stretching a web of Scotch tape over them. Then they sprayed some kind of plastic on the Scotch tape and formed an envelope. You've undoubtedly seen those. They put desiccants inside the envelope.* I have no idea how that worked out, but I suppose it worked. Mostly they had me scraping paint in places where you couldn't scrape paint.

I remember working on a telephone box which had all kinds of funny little angles in it. Then they got us down in damage control. We took up the deck plates in damage control, and they said, "You want to scrape the deck under the cables." I don't know if you've ever seen the situation in damage control on a big ship, but the cables were like spaghetti and they were everywhere. Here and there you could see beyond the cables. You could see some deck, and we were supposed to be scraping that deck. A bunch of us worked on it, and we gave it a try. But you couldn't really get your hands in. You could get the scraper in and try to wiggle it a little bit. It didn't make any sense at all. Somebody said, "What are we going to do after we've done scraping?"

"Well, we're going to chromate it."†

"Okay, we've done scraping. Let's chromate it." We went to the paint locker and we got buckets and buckets and buckets of chromate and we poured it in there. That's all we could do.

Q: You couldn't get a brush in.

Dr. Karpeles: Couldn't get a brush in. If somebody had had spray equipment it would have made some sense to spray it in, I suppose. It would have made more sense than pouring it, I'm sure. But I have visions of that stuff sloshing around in there yet, because it couldn't dry.

Q: Was there any time during this whole procedure that you had some misgivings about being so patriotic and getting drafted?

---

* Mothballed ships are equipped with dehumidification systems to minimize rust and corrosion of the interior.
† Zinc chromate is a primer put on before the top coat of paint.

Dr. Karpeles: I don't know. I talk about it now a little bit cynically, but I don't think I could have done anything else. That was the way I'd been raised. My father had gone to war in the First World War. He'd gone as a medical officer, and so it was firmly fixed in my mind that when the country was at war then you were at war too. That's all there was to it. Now, if I were back at the age of 21 again and it was Vietnam, I suppose I wouldn't have been that crazy. But I thought World War II was a necessary war. I still think it was a necessary war. I've never had much of an idea about dying. I don't yet, but I was willing to die for it, whatever that means. I would hate to have been faced with the certain knowledge that today is the day you're going to die. But in the abstract to sign up for whatever was to be signed up for, yes, I'd take my chances. If the same thing happened today I'd have the same attitude. I wouldn't be one of these 70-year-olds that goes down and tries to enlist, but I'd have the same feeling. Nothing they ask is too much.

Q: Well, you talked about putting aside money for medical school. Did you go into that after you were discharged?

Dr. Karpeles: Oh, yes. Actually, I didn't put aside enough for medical school. I wasn't saving for medical school. I was just saving. But I had $4,000 or $5,000 by the time I was out of the Navy. And I went into psychoanalysis somewhere in there. The day the atom bomb dropped I had two thoughts: A. The war is over; that's good. B. This is what physicists have done to the world; that's bad. I couldn't see spending my life trying to develop a better bomb.

So from that point I wasn't going to be a physicist; first I was going to be a biophysicist. I didn't quite know what it was, but I was going to be one anyhow. I went to Hopkins for a year with the idea of being a biophysicist. They were just about to open the department at that time. I was in danger of flunking out of graduate school at Hopkins and decided I really ought to get out before I flunked out. So I got out and went to work in a number of jobs that had technical stuff. Worked at GE X-ray, and that was a bummer, because I had a lousy boss and then I quit that.* I tried to do something on my own. That was a bummer, because I was much too stupid to start a business. Then I got a real nice job with the Coast Guard. I stayed with that while I was in analysis--the analyst got the money, and I had the fun.

Ultimately I came to the conclusion that I should have done what my father wanted me to do in the first place and study medicine. So I talked to my father about it and said, "I think I'd like to study medicine. I think I'd like to be a doctor. But I'm 29, [or whatever I was by that time], and it's hard to imagine that I'm going to go six years or whatever it takes and not develop any idea about getting married. I think I've got enough money to go to medical school, but I don't think I've got enough money to get married and go to medical school, so if I needed money could you help me out?"

He was delighted: "Of course, I'll help you out."

I said, "It may never come up, but if it does I'll let you know." I applied and got admitted to the University of Washington, Seattle. Then I wrote him a letter that I'd been admitted to the University of Washington Medical School.

He had had a series of strokes by that time, and he was way out of it. My sister was taking care of him, and she said he'd start out for the bathroom and forget where he was going before he got there. But he got the news I was admitted to medical school, and I got a phone call: "How much money do you need?" I've always wished I told him I could use $1,000, because I think he would have more fun writing out that check for $1,000 than anything he did in his life. But I didn't need any money, and I told him I didn't need any. He died not very long after that.

When I was at Hopkins, I used to come home and chat with him about what I was studying at Hopkins and the professors I had, and he was interested in everything. I'd come home on weekends, and we'd sit out in the kitchen and nosh and talk. It would have wonderful to have been able to share my agonies in medical school with him, and he would have enjoyed it.

---

* GE--General Electric.

Q: Did you ultimately become a physician?

Dr. Karpeles: I got my M.D., I did my internship, I got married. The lady that went out just a little while ago is my first wife. I inherited from my father just about enough money to get through, with the family and all. She was a good money manager; she took care of the money. We got through and went through internship. At the end of internship she said, "If you're going to do a residency, I'm leaving." Because she had a newborn and a two year old to take care of, and I was never home. And no money. It was killing her.

I said, "Okay, we'll check the alternatives." The alternative was a fellowship; I got a fellowship as a post-doctoral, and it paid enough to live on. It was in physiology, so I became a physiologist and a physiology professor in time. It all worked out very well for a long time, but she and I broke up. As you can see, there are no hard feelings involved. We did everything we could to see that the children were properly looked after. She and my present wife were friends before I ever thought of marrying Nancy, and they're still friends. She's been here helping Nancy with some sewing. Anyhow, I took the fellowship and became, as a result, a cardiovascular physiologist. I did that because I got tied up with a guy who was a big wheel in cardiovascular physiology.

After that I came back to Baltimore to teach cardiovascular physiology in medical school and did so for about 20 years at the University of Maryland. I loved teaching. I didn't like anything else about being on the faculty of a medical school, because it was a lot of infighting and a lot of fuss about publications; I wasn't publishing. I don't know, a lot of trouble.

Finally I decided that what I ought to do was go into practice, but I didn't decide it all of a sudden. I had almost unlimited freedom as a professor, and so I started spending my time on the cardiology division, rather than the cardiovascular. I was teaching cardiovascular physiology, but that wasn't the problem. I was attending all kinds of staff rounds in cardiology, and they were glad to have me because practicing cardiologists forget the physiology. They have a physiologist come in and make comments, just so he didn't talk too loud. That was okay.

Then I started making rounds with the family practice people, and I got my feet wet a little bit at a time. Finally, I went to my chairman and said, "I've been thinking I really ought to practice medicine. I was thinking of applying for an internship somewhere. Would you support me?"

He said, "Absolutely." Whether he wanted to get rid of me--I don't think he did, but he might have--or whether he just thought it was a good decision, I don't know. But he said he'd support me. So then I went to the chairman of family practice division, and I said, "I want to do this. Would you be able to give me recommendation?"

He said, "Absolutely. Tell me where you want to go and I'll recommend you."

I said, "Well, you've stuck yourself with a new resident, because I'm going right here." So I did my residency at the University of Maryland in from 1977 to 1980 and then went into practice up in Pennsylvania. It was a family practice, solo, cheapo. I had the advantage over everybody else I knew going into practice, because they all went in with $100,000 of debt, and I went in with a small pension and no debt.

I had formed ideas of how to practice medicine from watching my father and mother. It wasn't the way anybody practices medicine today, but that's what I did. I enjoyed it. I didn't have a big practice. I didn't have a rich practice. I was able to pay all the living expenses very comfortably. I didn't want to join a country club. I didn't want to drive a Cadillac. I loved making house calls. I had a ball. I got sick and had to quit after a while.

So the advantage of having to quit was that I'd known Nancy for some time by then. She was in Annapolis, and I was in Blue Ridge Summit. We were having a sort of commuting romance going on, which wasn't much good. I said, "Well, if I've got to quit I've got to quit. I'll go to Annapolis and get married." And so I did. I had a pension from the University of Maryland and Social Security, so I'm tolerably well fixed. I still don't have expensive tastes, so it works out fine. You've got the whole story of my life.

Q: A fascinating one, indeed--the versatility for one thing.

Dr. Karpeles: You know, I love being versatile. When I was in the Navy I loved hitting a new town and just make a liberty and walk around the streets and see what was to be seen. There was always something interesting. Seems to me like everywhere I go there's always something interesting, and I think I'm very fortunate. I don't know where that comes from, but it's a facility that I call a blessing for anybody that can have it.

Q: Well, any final thoughts by way of benediction on your associations with the Navy?

Dr. Karpeles: When I think back about my time in the Navy, it seems to me I was having a ball. When I was in the Navy, though, I wanted out real bad, because I wanted to get on with my life. I had never a thought of being a career Navy person, so this was an interruption in whatever the heck my life was going to be and I wanted out. But I had a lot of good times in the Navy and very few bad times. The biggest thing that bothered me was feeling like the percentage of incompetents that were around you was too high. I worry about that. Maybe the people they're turning out of Annapolis now are a different kettle of fish altogether; I don't know. Of course, most of the officers I was dealing with weren't out of Annapolis. It seemed to me too damn much was done with what the British call muddling through. The idea that you could understand what you were doing and that if you understood it there was a right way to do it and you didn't have to make a whole bunch of dumb mistakes to get there, didn't seem to be a widespread notion.

Q: Well, if we could just take the threat of magnetic mines as an example, it sounds from the time you've described it went from muddling through to doing it the right way.

Dr. Karpeles: Yes. But I heard that the _Alabama_ took only one hit in the whole war, and that was when one 5-inch mount fired into another 5-inch mount because somebody overrode the cutout.* Well, that was said to have been in the excitement of the kamikaze

---

* The incident occurred on 21 February 1944 while the _Alabama_ she was repelling a Japanese air attack. On the starboard side, 5-inch mount number nine fired into 5-inch mount number five. Five crew members were killed, another 11 were wounded.

attack, and I guess anybody can make a mistake. It's awfully easy to second guess. I think about that in the Waco business.* You know, sure the Waco business was handled wrong, but that's easy to say.

Q: In hindsight.

Dr. Karpeles: In hindsight. Pretty clear that whatever the hell we've done in Bosnia we haven't done it right.† But I couldn't have done it any better. I don't know what the hell we should have done.

Q: Well, I think Herman Wouk expressed it well in The Caine Mutiny.‡ He said, "The Navy is a system designed by geniuses to be executed by idiots."

Dr. Karpeles: [Laughter] I think that probably comes pretty close to it.

Q: On the whole things work well, but at times the idiot tendencies cause these problems.

Dr. Karpeles: Yes. What is your status?

Q: I'm a retired reserve officer, working as a civilian for the Naval Institute. When I was on active duty, I served in the New Jersey, a slightly more modern battleship than the Alabama. And I have to tell you that I have learned more this afternoon about ways of countering magnetic mines than during the entire time I was on active duty.

---

* In April 1993 agents from the Federal Bureau of Investigation stormed a compound held by members of a religious cult. The cult members set fire to the compound and burned to death rather than surrendering.
† In the mid-1990s the entities that had previously made up the nation of Yugoslavia waged a vicious civil war.
‡ Herman Wouk's classic naval novel of World War II, The Caine Mutiny, was published by Doubleday & Company in 1951.

Dr. Karpeles: What were you doing when you were on active duty?

Q: Mostly standing deck watches.

Dr. Karpeles: Well, I presume that engineering officers took care of degaussing, and deck officers assumed they knew what they were doing.

Q: That's right.

Dr. Karpeles: You hoped they knew what they were doing.

Q: We assumed it.
    Well, I thank you very much for your time. This information will be illuminating for those who use it.

Dr. Karpeles: Well, I'm at an age when running on is the best thing I do, and I've enjoyed it.

Q: Thank you very much.

Index To

Reminiscences of

Dr. Leo M. Karpeles

Accidents
    In 1944, on board the battleship Alabama (BB-60), one of her 5-inch gun mounts fired into another, killing five men, 61-62

Advancement of Enlisted Personnel
    Karpeles successfully passed the test for electrician's mate third class on board the battleship Alabama (BB-60) shortly after the end of World War II, 49-50

Alabama, USS (BB-60)
    Experienced a turnover in crew members after returning to the United States in the autumn of 1945, 48-49; role of the electrical division in the ship's interior communications, 49-54; the fire-alarm system was undependable, 51-52; living conditions on board ship, 52-54; inactivation and decommissioning in 1946, 54-56; in 1944 one of her 5-inch gun mounts fired into another, killing five men, 61-62

Boston Navy Yard
    Conducted deperming measures on various ships in early 1942 to reduce their susceptibility to magnetic mines, 8-23; the shipyard workers were not eager to contribute to the deperming process, 15

Boyd, Commander Thales S., USN (USNA, 1912)
    Service on the staff of the 14th Naval District in World War II, 29-30

Bureau of Ordnance
    Early in World War II, was involved in recruiting physicists to aid in the war effort, 3-5; connection with degaussing efforts, 5-9

Civil Service
    Pay of civilians working on mine countermeasures in Hawaii during World War II, 30; number of civilian physicists working on mine countermeasures at Pearl Harbor late in World War II, 39-40

Classified Information
    Was too often treated carelessly by Navy people during World War II, 23-24; Karpeles's work on classified instruction books for electronic equipment, 36-37

Coast Guard, U.S.
    In World War II Karpeles worked with the Coast Guard port captain at Honolulu, Hawaii, concerning arrangements to measure the magnetic signatures of commercial ships leaving the harbor, 25-26

Collisions
    The battleship Washington (BB-56) collided in February 1944 with the battleship Indiana (BB-58), 38

Commercial Ships
U.S. commercial ships made regular transits connecting Honolulu with San Francisco during World War II, 24-27; a ranging station at Honolulu checked the magnetic fields of merchant ships as they left the harbor in World War II, 25-27; the crews of commercial ships that made the run to Murmansk, Russia, in World War II were much concerned about the means of combating magnetic mines, 27-28

Compasses
Magnetic compasses and associated equipment were removed from ships undergoing the deperming process at the Boston Navy Yard in 1942, 18-19

Conscription
See Draft

Damage Control
In the period right after World War II, the fire-alarm system in the battleship Alabama (BB-60) was undependable, 51-52

Degaussing
Explanation of its role in protecting ships from magnetic mines, 5-7; deperming was clumsy and mostly unsuccessful early in World War II but got much better later, 6; deperming at the Boston Navy Yard in early 1942 involved wrapping coils around ships and applying electrical charges, 9-23; a station at Pearl Harbor conducted deperming measures on various ships in World War II, 17, 21, 37-38, 40-41; a ranging station at Honolulu checked the magnetic fields of merchant ships as they left the harbor in World War II, 25-27; value of degaussing for ships going to north Russia in World War II, 27-28

Draft
Karpeles's work for the Navy as a civilian physicist made him exempt from being drafted in World War II, 5, 44-46

Great Lakes (Illinois) Naval Training Station
Location of recruit training for Karpeles in 1945, 47

Honolulu, Hawaii
U.S. commercial ships made regular transits connecting Honolulu with San Francisco during World War II, 24-27; a ranging station at Honolulu checked the magnetic fields of merchant ships as they left the harbor in World War II, 26-27; recreation opportunities for civilian workers during World War II, 39; a magnetic detector for submarines operated outside Honolulu Harbor in World War II, 42-43

Karpeles, Dr. Leo M.
Education as a physicist in North Carolina and Pennsylvania in the late 1930s and early 1940s, 1-3, 6, 8; when the United States entered World War II in late 1941, he offered his services as a physicist, 1-3; early in the U.S. war effort, he contracted to work for

the Navy as a civilian physicist in Washington, D.C., 3-5; his role as a civilian physicist made him exempt from being drafted in World War II, 5, 44-46; work on deperming projects at the Boston Navy Yard in early 1942, 7-23; work on deperming projects at Honolulu and Pearl Harbor in World War II, 17, 24-45; enlistment and training in the Navy in 1945, 46-48; served 1945-46 in the crew of the battleship Alabama (BB-60), 48-56; parents of, 57-60; civilian career in medicine, 57-60; wives of, 59-60

Kirtley, Lieutenant Charles A., USN (Ret.)

While with the Bureau of Ordnance early in World War II, he was involved in recruiting physicists to aid in the war effort, 3-5

Leave and Liberty

Recreation opportunities for civilian workers in Honolulu, Hawaii, during World War II, 39

Midway, Battle of

People stationed in Hawaii breathed more easily following the U.S. victory in the Battle of Midway in June 1942, 34-35

Mines

The crews of commercial ships that made the run to Murmansk, Russia, in World War II were much concerned about the means of combating magnetic mines, 27-28; Pearl Harbor installed an acoustic range at Waipio Point late in World War II as part of the defense against acoustic mines, 35-36; development of acoustic mines, 36-37

See also Degaussing

Minesweepers

Steel-hulled minesweepers were sunk in the invasion of Normandy in June 1944, 28-29

Murmansk, Russia

The crews of commercial ships that made the run to Murmansk in World War II were much concerned about the means of combating magnetic mines, 27-28

Pay and Allowances

For a civilian physicist working under contract with the Bureau of Ordnance in World War II, 4-5, 10, 30, 33

Pearl Harbor, Oahu, Hawaii

Conducted deperming measures on various ships in World War II to reduce their susceptibility to magnetic mines, 17, 21, 37-38, 40-41; the U.S. Navy reported far less damage in the 1941 Japanese attack than actually happened, 24; after the attack, U.S. personnel moved into quarters vacated by Japanese who were interned, 31-32; people stationed in Hawaii breathed more easily following the U.S. victory in the Battle of Midway in June 1942, 34-35; installation of an acoustic range at Waipio Point late in World War II as part of the defense against acoustic mines, 35-36; work on instruction books for electronic equipment, 36-37; the battleship Washington (BB-56) arrived for temporary repairs after her collision in February 1944 with the battleship Indiana (BB-58), 38; large ammunition explosion on board tank landing ships in May 1944, 43-44

Pearl Harbor Navy Yard
Simulated sabotage on one dry dock during World War II, 41-42

Puget Sound Naval Shipyard, Bremerton, Washington
Inactivation of the battleship Alabama (BB-60) in 1946, 55-56

Recruit Training
At the Great Lakes Naval Training Station in 1945, 47

Soviet Union
The crews of commercial ships that made the run to Murmansk in World War II were much concerned about the means of combating magnetic mines, 27-28

Training
Of recruits at the Great Lakes Naval Training Station in 1945, 47; training in electronics in Chicago in 1945, 47-48

Washington, USS (BB-56)
Arrived at Pearl Harbor for temporary repairs after her collision in February 1944 with the battleship Indiana (BB-58), 38

www.ingramcontent.com/pod-product-compliance
Lightning Source LLC
Chambersburg PA
CBHW080610170426
43209CB00007B/1387